OUT & ABOUT

• WALKING GUIDES TO BRITAIN •

No 1

The Scottish Borders
and South West Highlands

MARSHALL CAVENDISH

From 1 April 1996, local authority boundaries in Scotland will change.
For up-to-date information, contact the relevant regional council
or the Scottish Office:

Dumfries & Galloway   (0387) 61234
Borders   (0835) 823301
Strathclyde   (041) 204 2900
Lothian   (031) 229 9292
Central   (0786) 442000
Fife   (0592) 754411
Scottish Office, Edinburgh   (031) 556 8400

First published in Great Britain in 1995 by
Marshall Cavendish Books, London
(a division of Marshall Cavendish Partworks Ltd)

Copyright © 1995 Marshall Cavendish

ISBN 03190 057 39

British Library Cataloguing in Publication Data:
A catalogue record for this book is available from the British Library

Printed and bound in Dubai, U.A.E.

Some of this material has previously appeared in the Marshall Cavendish partwork OUT & ABOUT

CONTENTS

Introduction to
OUT & ABOUT
• WALKING GUIDES TO BRITAIN •

Walking has become one of the most popular pastimes in Britain. To enjoy walking, you don't need any special skills, you don't have to follow rules or join expensive clubs, and you don't need any special equipment – though a pair of walking boots is a good idea! It is an easy way of relaxing and getting some exercise, and of enjoying nature and the changing seasons.

The OUT & ABOUT WALKING GUIDES TO BRITAIN will give you ideas for walks in your own neighbourhood and in other areas of Britain. All the walks are devised around a theme and range in length from about 2 to 9 miles (3.25 to 14.5 km) and in difficulty from very easy to mildly strenuous. Since each walk is circular, you will always be able to get back to your starting point.

Devised by experts and tested for accuracy, all the walks are accompanied by clear, practical instructions and an enlarged section of the relevant Ordnance Survey map. The flavour of the walk and highlights to look out for are described in the introductory text.

LOCAL COLOUR

Background features give you extra insight into items of local interest. The OUT & ABOUT WALKING GUIDES TO BRITAIN relate legends, point out unusual architectural details, provide a potted history of the lives of famous writers and artists connected with a particular place, explain traditional crafts still practised by local artisans, and uncover the secrets behind an ever-changing landscape.

DISCOVER NATURE

One of the greatest pleasures in going for a walk is the sense of being close to nature. On the walks suggested in the OUT & ABOUT WALKING GUIDES TO BRITAIN, you can feel the wind, smell the pine trees, hear the birds and see the beauty of the countryside. You will become more aware of the seasons – the life cycles of butterflies, the mating calls of birds, the protective behaviour of all creatures with their young. You will see the beginning of new life in the forests and fields, the bluebell carpets in spring woodlands, the dazzling beauty of rhododendron bushes in early summer, the swaying cornfields of summer and the golden colours of leaves in autumn. The OUT & ABOUT WALKING GUIDES TO BRITAIN tell you what to look out for and where to find it.

NATURE WALK

Occasional nature walk panels. will highlight an interesting feature that you will see on your walk. You will learn about natural and manmade details in the landscape, how to tell which animal or bird has nibbled the cones in a pine forest, what nurse trees are and what a triangulation point is.

ABOVE: *Colourful narrowboats are always an attractive feature on inland waterways.*

FACT FILE

The fact file will give you at-a-glance information about each walk to help you make your selection.

- ✳ **general location**
- **os** **map reference for Ordnance Survey**
- **map with grid reference for starting point**

| miles 0 | 1 | 2 | 3 | 4 | 5 | 6 | 7 | 8 | 9 | **length of the walk in** |
| kms 0 | 1 2 | 3 | 4 | 5 | 6 | 7 | 8 | 9 10 11 12 | 13 14 15 | **miles and kilometres** |

- ◔ **time needed if walking at an average speed**
- ▬ **character of the walk: easy/easy with**
- ◣ **strenuous parts/mildly strenuous; hills to**
- ▲ **be climbed and muddy or dangerous areas are pointed out**
- P **parking facilities near the start of the walk**
- T **public transport information**
- 🍺 **facilities for refreshment, including pubs**
- 🍴 **serving lunchtime meals, restaurants, tea rooms and picnic areas**
- WC **location of toilets**
- ⌘ **historic sites**

ORDNANCE SURVEY MAPS

All the walks in the OUT & ABOUT WALKING GUIDES TO BRITAIN are illustrated on large-scale, full-colour maps supplied by the Ordnance Survey. Ordnance Survey are justifiably proud of their worldwide reputation for excellence and accuracy. For extra clarity, the maps have been enlarged to a scale of 1:21,120 (3 inches to 1 mile).

The route for each walk is marked clearly on the map with a broken red line, and the numbers along the route refer you to the numbered stages in the written directions. In addition, points of interest are marked on the maps with letters. Each one is mentioned in the walk directions and is described in detail in the introductory text.

COUNTRYWISE

The countryside is one of our greatest resources. If we treat it with respect, we can preserve it for the future.

Throughout the countryside there is a network of paths and byways. Some are former trading routes, others are simply the paths villagers took to visit one another in the days before public transport. Most are designated 'rights of way': foot-paths, open only to people on foot, and bridleways, open to people on foot, horseback or bicycle. These paths can be identified on Ordnance Survey maps and verified, in cases of dispute, by the definitive map for the area, held by the relevant local authority.

THE LAW OF TRESPASS

If you find a public right of way barred to you, you may remove the obstruction or take a short detour around it. However, in England and Wales, if you stray from the footpath you are trespassing and could be sued in a civil court for damages. In Scotland, rights of way are not recorded on definitive maps, nor is there a law of trespass. Although you may cross mountain and moorland paths, landowners are permitted to impose restrictions on access, such as during the grouse-shooting season, which should be obeyed.

If you are following a public right of way and find, for example, that your path is blocked by a field of crops, you are entitled to walk the line of the footpath through the crops, in single file. Farmers are required, by law, to restore public rights of way within 14 days of ploughing. However, if you feel uncomfortable about doing this and can find a way round, then do so. But report the matter to the local authority who will take the necessary action to clear the correct route.

RIGHT: *The stunning patchwork of fields surrounding the picturesque village of Widecombe in the heart of Dartmoor makes a beautiful setting for the famous annual fair.*
BELOW: *Brown hares boxing in spring are a fascinating sight.*

It is illegal for farmers to place a bull on its own in a field crossed by a right of way (unless the bull is not a recognized dairy breed). If you come across a bull alone in a field, find another way round.

COMMONS AND PARKS

There are certain areas in England and Wales where you may be able to wander without keeping to paths, such as most commons and beaches. There are also country parks, set up by local authorities for public recreation – parkland, woodland, heath or farmland.

The National Trust is the largest private landowner in England and Wales. Its purpose is to preserve areas of natural beauty and sites of historic interest by acquisition, holding them in trust for public access and enjoyment. Information on access may be obtained from National Trust headquarters at

THE COUNTRY CODE

- **Enjoy the countryside, and respect its life and work**

- **Always guard against risk of fire**

- **Fasten all gates**

- **Keep your dogs under close control**

- **Keep to public footpaths across farmland**

- **Use gates and stiles to cross fences, hedges and walls**

- **Leave livestock, crops and machinery alone**

- **Take your litter home**

- **Help to keep all water clean**

- **Protect wildlife, plants and trees**

- **Take special care on country roads**

- **Make no unnecessary noise**

36 QueenAnne's Gate, London SW1H 9AS
Tel: 071-222 9251.

Most regions of great scenic beauty in England and Wales are designated National Parks or Areas of Outstanding Natural Beauty (AONB). In Scotland, they are known as National Scenic Areas (NSAs) or AONBs.

Most of this land is privately owned and there is no right of public access. In some cases, local authorities may have negotiated agreements with landowners to allow walkers access on mountains and moors.

CONSERVATION

National park, AONB or NSA status is intended to provide some measure of protection for the landscape, guarding against unsuitable development while encouraging enjoyment of its natural beauty.

ABOVE RIGHT *Carelessness with cigarettes, matches or camp fires can be devastating in a forest.*

Nature reserves are areas set aside for conservation. Most are privately owned, some by large organizations such as the Royal Society for the Protection of Birds. Although some offer public access, most require permission to enter.

THE RAMBLERS ASSOCIATION

The aims of the Ramblers Association are to further greater understanding and care of the countryside, to protect and enhance public rights of way and areas of natural beauty, to improve public access to the countryside, and to encourage more people to take up rambling as a healthy, recreational activity. It has played an important role in preserving and developing our national footpath network.

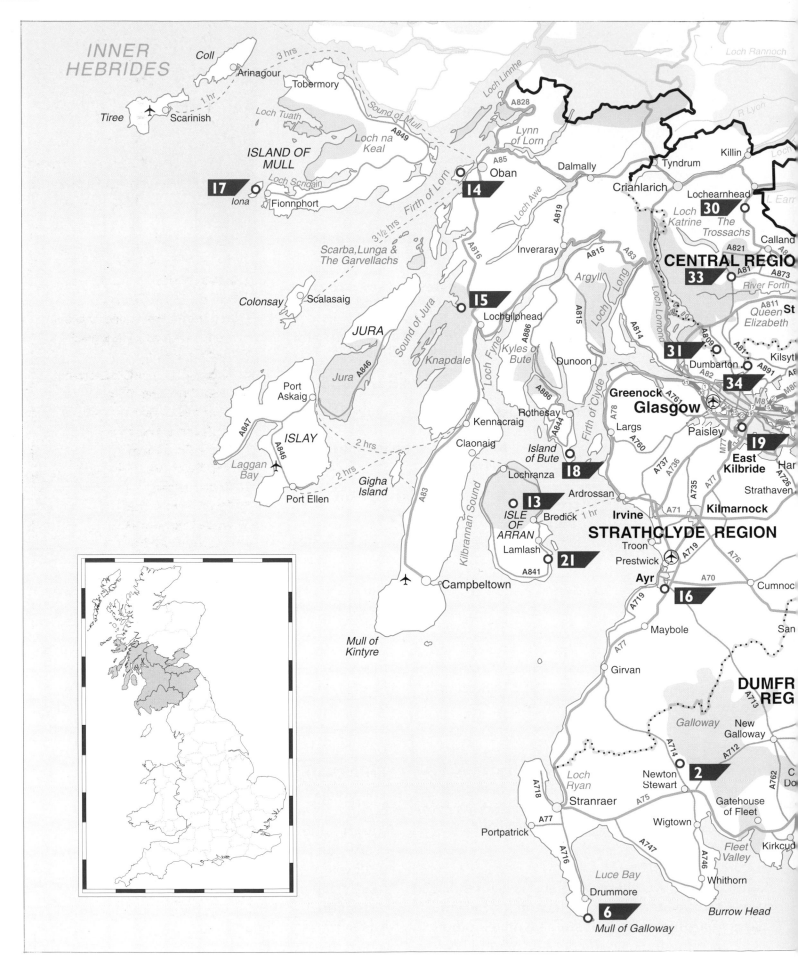

INNER HEBRIDES

Coll
Arinagour
Tobermory

3 hrs
1 hr

Tiree
Scarinish

Loch Rannoch

Loch Linnhe
A828

Lynn of Lorn

Loch Tuath

Sound of Mull

A849

Loch na Keal

ISLAND OF MULL

Loch Scridain

17
Iona
Fionnphort

Firth of Lorn

14
Oban

A85

Dalmally

Loch Awe

A819

Killin

Tyndrum

Crianlarich

Lochearnhead

L. Earn

30
Loch Katrine
The Trossachs

Calland

Scarba, Lunga & The Garvellachs

3½ hrs

A816

Inveraray

A815

A83

Argyll

A821

CENTRAL REGIO
33
A81
A873

River Forth

Colonsay
Scalasaig

15
Lochgilphead

A815

A814

Loch Lomond

Loch Fyne

A811

Queen St Elizabeth

JURA

Sound of Jura

Jura A846

Knapdale

Kyles of Bute

A886

Dunoon

31

A809

Dumbarton

A82

Kilsyt

A891

34

A847

Port Askaig

Rothesay

A844

Firth of Clyde

A78

Greenock
Glasgow

A761

Paisley

Kilsyt

ISLAY

A846

Laggan Bay

Kennacraig

Claonaig

2 hrs

Island of Bute

Largs

A760

M8

19

A847

East Kilbride

Har

Port Ellen

Gigha Island

2 hrs

18
Lochranza

13
ISLE OF ARRAN
Bredick

1 hr

Ardrossan

A78

Strathaven

A737

A735

A726

A71

Kilbrannan Sound

A83

Lamlash

21
A841

STRATHCLYDE REGION

Irvine

Kilmarnock

Troon
Prestwick

A719

A76

Mull of Kintyre

Campbeltown

Ayr

16
A719

A70

Cumnoc

Maybole

San

A77

Girvan

DUMFR REG

Galloway
New Galloway

A713

A762

2
Newton Stewart
A714
A712

C Do

Loch Ryan

A718

Stranraer

Gatehouse of Fleet

Portpatrick
A77

A75

Wigtown

A747

A746

Fleet Valley

Kirkcud

A716

Luce Bay

Whithorn

Drummore

6
Mull of Galloway

Burrow Head

The Scottish Borders & South West Highlands

All the walks featured in this book are plotted and numbered on the regional map (left) and listed in the box below.

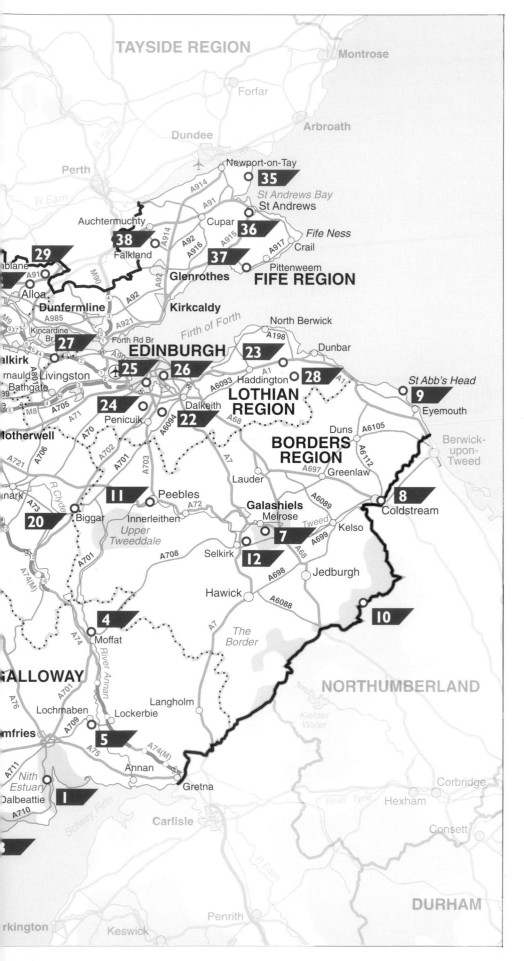

USING MAPS

Although the OUT & ABOUT WALKING GUIDES TO BRITAIN give you all the information you need, it is useful to have some basic map skills. Most of us have some experience of using a motoring atlas to navigate by car. Navigating when walking is much the same, except that mistakes are much more time and energy consuming and, if circumstances conspire, could lead to an accident.

A large-scale map is the answer to identifying where you are. Britain is fortunate in having the best mapping agency in the world, the Ordnance Survey, which produces high-quality maps, the most popular being the 1:50,000 Landranger series. However, the most useful for walkers are the 1:25,000 Pathfinder, Explorer and Outdoor Leisure maps.

THE LIE OF THE LAND

A map provides more than just a bird's eye view of the land; it also conveys information about the terrain – whether marshy, forested, covered with tussocky grass or boulders; it distinguishes between footpaths and bridleways; and shows boundaries such as parish and county boundaries.

Symbols are used to identify a variety of land-marks such as churches, camp and caravan sites, bus, coach and rail stations, castles, caves and historic houses. Perhaps most importantly of all, the shape of the land is indicated by contour lines. Each line represents land at a specific height so it is possible to read the gradient from the spacing of the lines (the closer the spacing, the steeper the hill).

GRID REFERENCES

All Ordnance Survey maps are over-printed with a framework of squares known as the National Grid. This is a reference system which, by breaking the country down into squares, allows you to pinpoint any place in the country and give it a unique reference number; very useful when making rendezvous arrangements. On OS Landranger, Pathfinder and Outdoor Leisure maps it is possible to give a reference to an accuarcy of 100 metres. Grid squares on these maps cover an area of 1 km x 1 km on the ground.

GIVING A GRID REFERENCE

Blenheim Palace in Oxfordshire has a grid reference of **SP 441 161**. This is constructed as follows:

SP These letters identify the 100 km grid square in which Blenheim Palace lies. These squares form the basis of the National Grid. Information on the

100 km square covering a particular map is always given in the map key.

441 161 This six figure reference locates the position of Blenheim Palace to 100 metres in the 100 km grid square.

44 This part of the reference is the number of the grid line which forms the western (left-hand) boundary of the 1 km grid square in which Blenheim Palace appears. This number is printed in the top and bottom margins of the relevant OS map (Pathfinder 1092 in this case).

16 This part of the reference is the number of the grid line which forms the southern (lower) boundary of the 1 km grid square in which Blenheim Palace appears. This number is printed in the left- and right-hand margins of the relevant OS map (Pathfinder 1092).

These two numbers together (SP 4416) locate the bottom left-hand corner of

the 1 km grid square in which Blenheim Palace appears. The remaining figures in the reference **441 161** pinpoint the position within that square by dividing its western boundary lines into tenths and estimating on which imaginary tenths line Blenheim Palace lies.

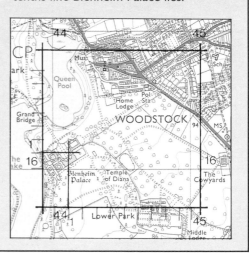

THE NITH ESTUARY

◄*New Abbey village lies west of the River Nith and its estuary, which runs into the Solway Firth.*

PETER DAVENPORT/EDINBURGH PHOTOGRAPHIC LIBRARY. INSET: L. CAMPBELL/NHPA

FACT FILE

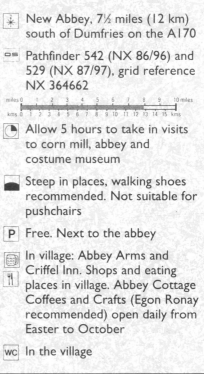

※ New Abbey, 7½ miles (12 km) south of Dumfries on the A170

OS Pathfinder 542 (NX 86/96) and 529 (NX 87/97), grid reference NX 364662

miles 0 1 2 3 4 5 6 7 8 9 10 miles
kms 0 1 2 3 4 5 6 7 8 9 10 11 12 13 14 15 kms

◔ Allow 5 hours to take in visits to corn mill, abbey and costume museum

⬛ Steep in places, walking shoes recommended. Not suitable for pushchairs

P Free. Next to the abbey

🏨 In village: Abbey Arms and Criffel Inn. Shops and eating places in village. Abbey Cottage Coffees and Crafts (Egon Ronay recommended) open daily from Easter to October

WC In the village

◄*The brambling is one of the finch family and its habitat is woods and farmland. New Abbey's corn mill (below) is in working order and is regularly demonstrated to visitors.*

JOHN WATNEY

Through a National Scenic Area overlooking Solway Firth

Few villages in south-west Scotland are as attractive as New Abbey, which is by the Nith Estuary and below mighty Criffel — the popular hill nicknamed 'the Sentinel of the South'. The walk leads alongside Kirkconnell Flow ⓓ. This is a rare example of a raised peat bog that has been colonized by Scots pines and birch trees and is protected by the Nature Conservancy Council as a National Nature Reserve.

UNSPOILT COUNTRY

The route is almost exclusively on tarmac roads, but this in no way diminishes its attraction, since this corner of Scotland is relatively unspoilt. In spring and summer there is an abundance of foliage and greenery and on crisp winter mornings the area takes on a charm of a different sort.

New Abbey owes its name to the last monastery to be built on the Scottish mainland. It dominates one of 40 areas in Scotland designated in 1978 as National Scenic Areas (usually referred to as NSAs).

The Nith Estuary NSA is an extensive landscape of mud flats, with sand banks and salt merses (marshes) teeming with wildlife. It is fringed by deciduous copses and fertile lowlands and criss-crossed with sturdy Galloway stone dykes. It is also part of the Solway Firth Site of Special Scientific Interest that runs round the valley and across to England.

In the 18th century, Robert Burns, Scotland's national poet, worked here as an excise man and it was the arena for many of the scenes in Sir Walter Scott's Waverley novels, published in the 19th century. The village of Glencaple, across the estuary, was once a formidable ship building centre and it is still the heartland of haaf-net fishermen. They have continued to practise their craft of deep-sea fishing, unique to the Solway Firth, since the days of the Vikings.

KIRKCONNELL HOUSE

The best views of Kirkconnell Flow are from the brow of the road at Whinny Hill. See it close at hand from the enchanting route from the main Dumfries to New Abbey road to Kirkconnell House **E**. The latter is a narrow, 2-mile (3.2-km) avenue of ancient oaks where a car would be considered a traffic jam. Do not be put off by the gateposts at the junction — they seem to indicate a

private road, but it is public.

Kirkconnell House is Scotland's second oldest inhabited house and Galloway's oldest. Unfortunately it is not open to the public. The house has been in the hands of the Maxwell family for many generations. One of the family's prized

▶ *Shambellie House is in a forest of Scots Pines, which were planted as part of the Shambellie Estate between 1775 and 1780.*

BOTH PHOTOS JOHN WATNEY

◀*The 18th-century grey stone bridge crosses New Abbey Pow, the stream that runs through the village of New Abbey.*

possessions is a written copy of the prayer said to have been uttered by Mary, Queen of Scots as she ascended the scaffold. Tradition has it that Highlanders made clubs from the oak trees along the avenue to Kirkconnell House during the 1745 Jacobite Revolution, which could

THE WALK

NEW ABBEY KIRKCONNNELL

The walk begins in the car park outside Sweetheart Abbey Ⓐ in the village of New Abbey.

1 From the abbey car park walk down to the main street of the village and bear right along the street towards Dumfries. Cross the road at the village square to New Abbey Corn Mill Ⓑ, which stands between the Abbey Arms and the road bridge over New Abbey Pow. The working mill is open to visitors.

2 Cross the bridge and keep on the right side of this relatively busy road (the A710) past a church. Walk about 100 yards (90 metres) past the signpost to Beeswing, Kinharvie, Dumfries and Dalbeattie, to the sign for Shambellie House Museum of Costume Ⓒ, on the left. Cross the

road to visit the museum.

3 On leaving the museum cross the road again to face the oncoming traffic. There is a lodge-house on the left. Walk along the road for about 2 miles (3.2 km) up steep Whinny Hill and down the other side. There are superb views of the Solway Firth and Lake District peaks from the highest point of the road.

4 Turn sharp right at the bottom of Whinny Hill down the long avenue leading to Kirkconnell House Ⓔ. Kirkconnell Flow Ⓓ lies to the left. At the gate for Kirkconnell House, follow the road sharp right up towards New Abbey past Airds Farm road-end.

5 Continue along this narrow, winding road, which goes up and down for almost 1 mile (1.6 km), until the T-junction is reached. From this road there are fine views out to

sea and north-west to Criffel. Between Bogside Cottage and Shaw Cottage, the road is at its most undulating. Between Drummillan and Whiteneuk the road climbs steeply.

6 Take the left fork along the road headed by a dead-end sign. Do not take the road that leads down past Shambellie Grange to New Abbey. The route, another very narrow tree-lined one, leads to Landis Farm. There is a conveniently placed seat which is an excellent viewpoint for the abbey, Waterloo Monument Ⓖ, Criffel and Loch Kindar.

7 Continue along Landis Road which turns extremely sharply right down towards the village. A visit to the ruins of Abbot's tower Ⓕ, adjacent to the farm is recommended.

8 Proceed down the road, which becomes a dirt

track past the Maryfield Farm turn-off. Walk down to the foot-bridge in order to cross the New Abbey Pow. Follow the rough path to the right to the first wooden kissing gate (a bit careworn, but nevertheless a kissing gate). Go through and proceed to second gate.

9 Proceed a short distance along the track down a fence-line to a metal kissing gate on your left. Go through and follow the track straight down to the village next to well-built stone dyke. The path continues along the touchline of the village football field and becomes a narrow lane between a school and St Mary's Roman Catholic Church.

10 When you reach the street, turn right and follow the road until the sign for Sweetheart Abbey. Turn right into the car park.

JOHN WATNEY

◄*Kirkconnell Flow is not a river, as its name might suggest. Flow is a Scottish term for an area of land like a moor. Kirkconnell Merse is the marsh nearby.*

Year's Day hangovers. Given the right weather conditions the distant shapes of the Isle of Man and Arran can be seen from its top. Loch Kindar can be spotted at the foot of Criffel. The loch has two islets, the larger one being Kirk Kindar, which is reputed to have been a Celtic religious site and the site of the palace of Cendaeladh, a Pictish King. Somewhat further along the route, the ruins of Abbot's Tower **F** stand by Landis farm.

COSTUME MUSEUM

On the outskirts of New Abbey is the unique Shambellie House Museum of Costume **C**, a gift to the nation in 1977 by a local landowner, Charles Stewart. This late-Victorian baronial country house holds exhibitions drawing on the National Museums of Scotland's outstanding collection of costumes. The museum is open from May to September and admission is free.

account for why many of the trees branch out so near the ground.

The profusion of broad-leaved trees is one of the features that makes the walk so pleasant. Ivy-clad oaks line the steep road that meanders between the Airds Farm road-end to the T-junction.

GALLOWAY AIR

Enjoy a well-earned rest on the seat by the road from Shambellie Grange to Landis Farm and take a bracing draught of good Galloway air before doing the final lap of the walk. The

seat is a wonderful viewpoint. Rosy sandstone Sweetheart Abbey **A** stands forlornly, but proudly, in the foreground and the huge granite walls of the abbey precinct glint in sunlight. Above the village stands Criffel and to the right the Waterloo Monument **G**, a round tower 50 feet (30 metres) high, erected between Glen Craig and Carsegowan to commemorate the historic British victory against Napoleon in 1815.

Criffel Hill is a well-loved local landmark, celebrated as a traditional venue for fresh air to relieve New

▲*The Nith Estuary seen from Criffel Hill. Fishermen with haaf-nets (from the Norwegian for heave) continue their traditional craft in the estuary waters.*

The late 18th-century New Abbey Corn Mill **B** stands a stone's throw away next to the 1715 bridge over the New Abbey Pow (stream). It used to grind oatmeal for human consumption and other cereals for livestock. The water-powered mill worked until World War II and was recently restored. It belongs to the Scottish Development Department and is still in working order.

Sweetheart Abbey

Lady Devorgilla built Sweetheart Abbey in 1273 as a memorial to her beloved husband, John Balliol. A direct descendent of King David I, she carried his embalmed heart (her 'sweet, silent companion') around with her in a silver casket at all times.

When Lady Devorgilla died at the age of 80 in 1290, John Balliol's heart was buried with her. She endowed Balliol College, Oxford, which her husband had built, and she was responsible for building Dumfries' first bridge.

The Cistercian monks called the abbey *Dulce Cor* (Latin for sweet heart) in memory of Devorgilla's love. The building survived the Reformation thanks to the influence of the Maxwell family, but it was nearly pulled down in the 18th century. In 1779, some local gentlemen, including the parish minister, redeemed it for a small sum raised by public subscription.

Although Sweetheart Abbey now has no roof and few walls left, its imposing ruins make it an impressive site and the romantic story attached to it adds to its charm.

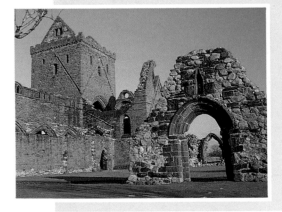

JOHN WATNEY

THE GLEN TROOL TRAIL

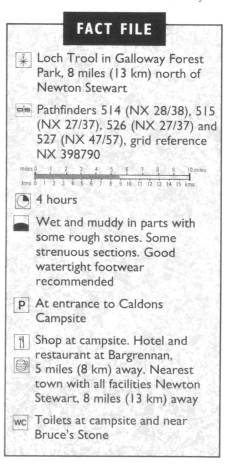

Further on is an area at the base of an escarpment called the Steps of Trool ⓓ. It was here, in 1307, that an English army was ambushed by King Robert the Bruce. The Scots, up on the slopes of Mulldonach, sent an avalanche of boulders down on them. Their success aided the campaign for independence for Scotland, which was finally won at Bannockburn in 1314.

LIGHTNING STRIKE

Today, the path picks its way through a landscape of big boulders. These are not those thrown by the ancient Scots; they were flung there by a lightning strike on a head of rock above. From here there is a clear view over the loch to the 2,770-foot (844-metre) summit of Merrick, which is the highest hill in the Southern Uplands.

Leaving the waterside, the walk turns north and steeply up to the high escarpment along the north flank of the loch. On the way it

JOHN WATNEY. INSET: HEATHER ANGEL

▲*Bruce's Stone overlooks Loch Trool. The Steps of Trool, where a battle was fought in the 14th century, are visible beyond the Loch. The Japanese larch grows its seeds in cones (left).*

A spectacular woodland walk at the feet of great hills

Set in the heart of the Galloway Forest Park, this walk offers fine vistas of the waters of Loch Trool ⓐ and the steep heights encircling Glen Trool. The view over the Loch from Bruce's Stone ⓕ, at the summit of the walk, is certainly one of Scotland's scenic jewels.

The Martyr's Tomb ⓑ, near the start of the walk, is a headstone within stone walls bearing the inscription 'Here lie James and Robert Duns, Thomas and John Stevenson, James McClive and

Andrew McCall who were surprised at prayer'. The people described were Presbyterians, or Covenanters (who took their name from the National Covenant signed in Edinburgh in 1638 and whose numbers were strongest in south-west Scotland), and they were persecuted by Charles I. Also carved on the headstone are the names of the soldiers who killed them.

18TH-CENTURY TREES

The walk passes through a campsite (stick to the marked path here), spread out in a most attractive park of oaks, then climbs up through a larch plantation and a wood of old Scots pines with their reddish bark. These trees were planted in the 18th century. The route loops round the high point called Torr ⓒ, leaving the old bridle-path in favour of one nearer the lochside.

FACT FILE

☀ Loch Trool in Galloway Forest Park, 8 miles (13 km) north of Newton Stewart

🗺 Pathfinders 514 (NX 28/38), 515 (NX 27/37), 526 (NX 27/37) and 527 (NX 47/57), grid reference NX 398790

```
miles 0  1  2  3  4  5  6  7  8  9  10 miles
kms 0 1 2 3 4 5 6 7 8 9 10 11 12 13 14 15 kms
```

🕐 4 hours

▬ Wet and muddy in parts with some rough stones. Some strenuous sections. Good watertight footwear recommended

🅿 At entrance to Caldons Campsite

🍴 Shop at campsite. Hotel and restaurant at Bargrennan, 5 miles (8 km) away. Nearest town with all facilities Newton Stewart, 8 miles (13 km) away

🚻 Toilets at campsite and near Bruce's Stone

THE WALK

GLEN TROOL

The walk begins from the car park at the south-west tip of Loch Trool Ⓐ.

➡ **1** Take the footpath on

it instead of the path back to the car park.

➡ **2** From the shop, walk to the far end of the site

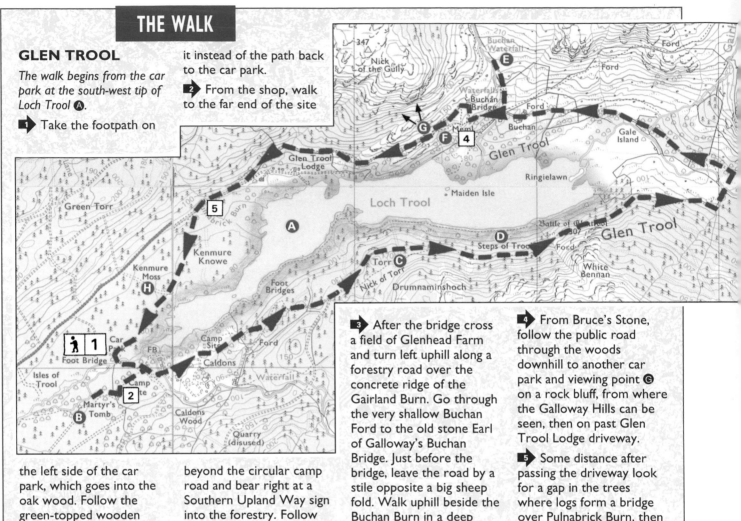

➡ **3** After the bridge cross a field of Glenhead Farm and turn left uphill along a forestry road over the concrete ridge of the Gairland Burn. Go through the very shallow Buchan Ford to the old stone Earl of Galloway's Buchan Bridge. Just before the bridge, leave the road by a stile opposite a big sheep fold. Walk uphill beside the Buchan Burn in a deep ravine for about 300 yards (275 metres) to the start of the Buchan Falls Ⓔ. Return to the forest road and continue uphill to the car park and Bruce's Stone Ⓕ, set high on a promontory overlooking the Loch.

➡ **4** From Bruce's Stone, follow the public road through the woods downhill to another car park and viewing point Ⓖ on a rock bluff, from where the Galloway Hills can be seen, then on past Glen Trool Lodge driveway.

➡ **5** Some distance after passing the driveway look for a gap in the trees where logs form a bridge over Pulnabrick Burn, then walk along a stone path down through Kenmure Moss Ⓗ. Follow the waymarks as before. The last stretch is a trodden path beside the Water of Trool leading to the road bridge by the car park from where the walk started.

the left side of the car park, which goes into the oak wood. Follow the green-topped wooden waymarks (crossing a small bridge) and, where the path joins the one from the campsite, turn right. Follow the paved pathway to the Martyr's Tomb Ⓑ. Return the same way, until you reach the path signposted to the campsite shop. Take

beyond the circular camp road and bear right at a Southern Upland Way sign into the forestry. Follow the bridlepath waymarks all the way through the Scots pine wood, round the Torr Ⓒ and across the Steps of Trool Ⓓ to reach the eastern limit of the trail at the wooden footbridge, which crosses over the Glenhead Burn.

passes through the ancient oak-woods of Glenhead and Buchan, which are of the sessile variety with distinctively stalked leaves. These woods are Sites of Special Scientific Interest and have been undisturbed since 1900, when they were coppiced to supply tan bark and wood for charcoal.

PANORAMIC HILLS

The Buchan Falls Ⓔ flow down through three suspended pools, in a deep, rock ravine softened by a thick coat of brilliant green mosses. These falls are very pretty and only a few

▶ *Buchan Burn runs for 3 miles (4.8 km) from its source before plunging down Buchan Falls, then into Loch Trool.*

moments' walk off the ascending path to Bruce's Stone, which looks across the Loch from a great height to the Steps of Trool battlefield. Near the stone is the start of a tough 4-mile (7.4-km) path to the summit of Merrick. From the stone, and also from a rock bluff further along the trail, the splendour of the Galloway Hills Ⓖ can be seen. Finally, at Kenmure Moss Ⓗ, there is a fine and varied plantation of trees.

JOHN WATNEY

ALISTAIR FIRTH/SCOTLAND IN FOCUS. INSET: G.W. WARD/AQUILA

◀*In a Bible story, Lot's wife was turned into a pillar of salt. The tall sea stack by Balcary Point is named after her. The razorbill (above) lives in sheltered crevices on the cliff face.*

following the death of Bruce.

In the 18th century, the island was the centre of a considerable smuggling trade and its caves were used to store the contraband. Smuggling reached such extensive proportions that in 1721 the King's cutter was stationed in Balcary Bay to police the area. It seemed to do little good, for in 1761 the Collector of Excise made a report that smugglers rode through the countryside

Around cliff tops to visit a fine sea-bird colony

As well as nesting sea-birds and spectacular cliffs, there is plenty more to see on this varied walk. The bracken and tall grasses of this south-facing coastline provide a sheltered haven for a variety of butterflies and moths. Inland there are quiet woods, both deciduous and coniferous. Historically thriving with shipping, industry, mining, smuggling and conflict, this area now retains only its rich flora and fauna, its quiet beauty and a few clues to its turbulent past. The writer Samuel Crockett (1860-1914) frequently visited this area and his novel *The Raiders* was set here.

The poles and nets stretching out into Balcary Bay belong to Balcary Fishery ⓐ, known locally as Fish Green. Stake-net fishing, established here in the mid-19th century, is still carried out today. In the early 1900s, a royal sturgeon measuring 9 feet (2.7 metres) was caught here.

FORTIFIED MANSION

At the mouth of the bay and the limit of the low-water mark is Hestan Island ⓑ. It houses an automatic lighthouse and a holiday cottage. A fortified mansion, the ruins of which remain, was built in 1342 by the unpopular John Balliol, who was crowned king of Scotland

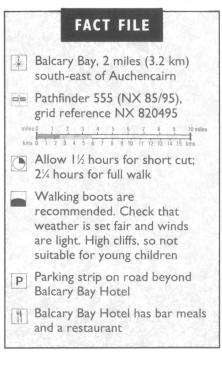

FACT FILE

- ✳ Balcary Bay, 2 miles (3.2 km) south-east of Auchencairn

- ▱ Pathfinder 555 (NX 85/95), grid reference NX 820495

  miles 0 1 2 3 4 5 6 7 8 9 10 miles
  kms 0 1 2 3 4 5 6 7 8 9 10 11 12 13 14 15 kms

- ◕ Allow 1½ hours for short cut; 2¼ hours for full walk

- ▬ Walking boots are recommended. Check that weather is set fair and winds are light. High cliffs, so not suitable for young children

- Ⓟ Parking strip on road beyond Balcary Bay Hotel

- 🍴 Balcary Bay Hotel has bar meals and a restaurant

THE WALK

BALCARY BAY

The walk starts at the parking strip opposite the wall of Balcary Bay Hotel gardens and cottages.

1 Follow the road until

Needle Rock

Manor House (remains of)

Hestan Island Caves **B**

Daft Ann's Steps

Balcary Fishery **A**

Balcary Bay

Balcary Bay Hotel

Airds Cottage

Tower House

Balcary Point

Balcary Hill

Lot's Wife **D**

Dorey Heu Wood

E

7

Quarry (dis)

Big Airds Hill

fort △102

Little Airds Hill

Mine (disused)

Sheepfold Homestead

Shaft (dis)

Airds Heugh

Lochenling

6

Door of the Heugh Adam's Chair

5

Airds Point

8

C

3

2

4

Hill and Little Airds Hill. At this point you can take a short cut – go through kissing gate on right and take a path through open fields, which leads back directly to the lane at the start of the walk.

5 Otherwise, continue along the coast to Airds Point then along above Airds Heugh and Rascarrel Bay to reach the edge of a conifer wood.

6 Turn right to follow along the burn and the edge of the wood, bearing right slightly along a retaining wall to cross a stile and gain the edge of Loch Mackie **E**.

7 Turn right to follow the path alongside the dyke to a gate next to a derelict cottage on your left. Continue through this, passing the house on your right and two further little woods before emerging on the road. Turn right to reach the car park and starting point.

the point where it turns a right angle (the point where the road rounds the corner of the cottages and makes a short descent into Balcary Bay). Continue straight on here, leaving surfaced road in favour of wooded lane. Shortly this leads to an open field.

2 Go through the gate and turn left (signpost) to cross the field with a house

on your left. Continue across the field until, at its far side, a kissing gate leads to a footpath through a wood. From the field there are views across Balcary Bay of Balcary Fishery **A** and Hestan Island **B**.

3 Follow the path passing the landscaped rock garden of Tower House on the left. Continue rising slightly until at a point emerging

from the wood the old Lifeboat Station **C** can be seen down below on the shore to the left.

4 Continue along the path to skirt the edge of the cliffs that form Balcary Point. In a little way the sea stack of Lot's Wife **D** can be seen. Continue along the coastal path to drop down slightly to the shoulder between Balcary

---

with upwards of sixty horses. In 1791 it was estimated that goods from five ships alone were valued at over £7,000. Balcary House (now the Balcary Bay Hotel) is said to have been constructed entirely from the proceeds of its smuggling trade.

The Lifeboat Station **C** at Balcary Point is now abandoned. The last boat to sail from here was called the *David Hay* and had a crew of around a dozen local men. During the nesting season (April to July), the cliffs of the point itself are alive with the sight and sound of sea birds. Many gulls nest here, including kittiwakes, fulmars, guillemots and razorbills. Look out for Lot's Wife **D**, a sea stack around 80 feet (25 metres) high and a nesting site.

In summer, the small copper, small blue, meadow brown and

large white butterflies may be seen flying amongst the luxuriant foliage and flowers further along the cliff tops. Look out too for the spectacularly coloured red and white magpie moth. Nearer the woods, the ringlet butterfly can be seen.

COPPER ORE

Before you reach the Forestry Commission fir trees of what was once Rascarrel Moss, you will see the remnants of an old barytes (barium sulphate) mine. Nearby, copper and coal have both been mined commercially in the past. In 1845, 60 tons (59 tonnes) of copper ore per week was shipped from Balcary Bay

▶ *The slipway of the disused Lifeboat Station juts out towards Hestan Island, 1,100 yards (1 km) away.*

to Birmingham. The surrounds of Loch Mackie **E** are home to both red and roe deer. On the water itself, the red throated diver and grebe are likely visitors here. The loch is owned by the McCrae family of Airds of Balcary and the Gilroy family of Auchencairn House. The path now leads easily through rich farming land. Finally you pass the ruined Airds Cottage and return to the starting point of the walk.

ALISTAIR FIRTH/SCOTLAND IN FOCUS

MOFFAT'S MAGIC WATERS

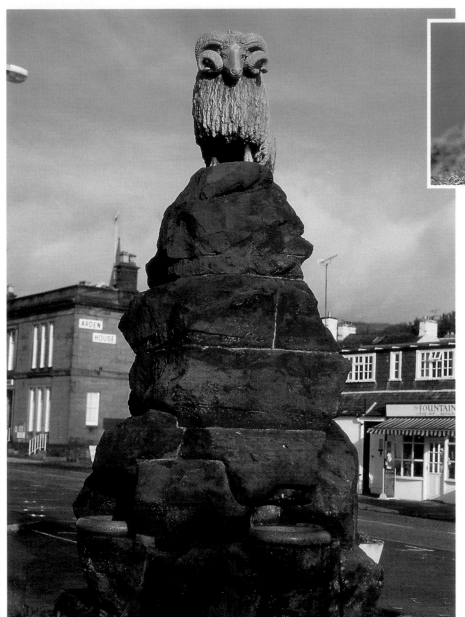

JASON SMALLEY. INSET: NATURE PHOTOGRAPHERS LTD

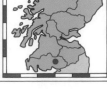

◀ *In the High Street, the Ram Statue, standing on a rock plinth that incorporates drinking fountains, is a notable landmark. The raven (above) is a bird of the surrounding hills.*

The walk begins at Station Park **A**, one reason why the town has twice won the 'Best Kept Village in Scotland' award in the Britain in Bloom competition. The park has a putting green and a popular boating pond. It also contains a memorial to Moffat-born Air Marshal Lord Dowding, who directed Fighter Command in the Battle of Britain.

The High Street has a number of attractions, among them the Star Hotel, the narrowest detached hotel in Britain. Beside the hotel is the old graveyard **B**, where John Loudon Macadam, the civil engineer who

Around an historic spa town and to the woods and hills beyond

The spa town of Moffat huddles among the smooth hills that typify the scenery of northern Dumfriesshire. Today, Moffat's mineral waters are drunk only by the occasional daring visitor, but in the 18th and 19th centuries the town was a fashionable health resort for the middle and upper classes.

Rachel Whiteford, daughter of the then Bishop of Moffat, discovered Moffat Well, a sulphur spring, in 1633, while the iron-bearing waters of Hartfell Spa were discovered in 1748. Those who partook of the 'magic waters' from the springs included Scotland's bard, Robert Burns; David Hume, the philosopher; John Home, the playwright; James Boswell, the amanuensis of Dr Johnson; and James McPherson, who duped the literary world by passing off his poetry as the work of Ossian, a Celtic mystic.

FACT FILE

✳	Moffat, 13 miles (21km) north of Lockerbie off the A74 Glasgow to Carlisle road
OS	Pathfinder 495 (NY 00/10), grid reference NY 084050

miles 0 1 2 3 4 5 6 7 8 9 10 miles
kms 0 1 2 3 4 5 6 7 8 9 10 11 12 13 14 15 kms

◕	Allow 2 hours
▬	Some steep climbs and wet in places. Walking boots recommended
P	Opposite Station Park (free)
⑂	A good selection of cafés and pubs
WC	Next to Town Hall

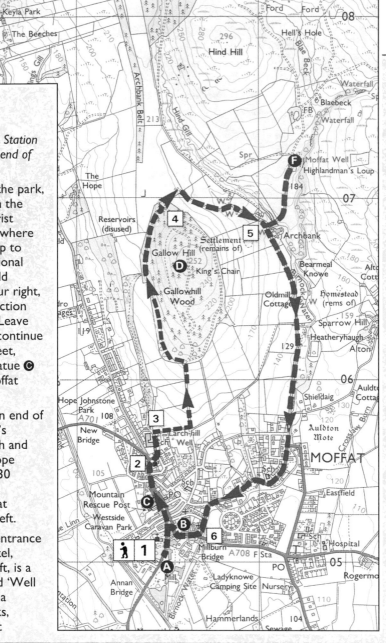

MOFFAT

The walk starts from Station Park Ⓐ at the south end of Moffat on the A701.

▶1 Having visited the park, head north through the town, past the tourist information office (where you may like to stop to pick up some additional literature) to the old graveyard Ⓑ on your right, just beyond the junction with Selkirk Road. Leave the graveyard and continue up Moffat High Street, passing the Ram Statue Ⓒ and the narrow Moffat House Hotel.

▶2 At the northern end of town, pass St Mary's United Free Church and cut right up Harthope Place. After about 30 paces, bear left and continue past Moffat Academy on your left.

▶3 Opposite the entrance to Beechwood Hotel, which is on your left, is a footpath signposted 'Well Road'. Follow it to a crossroads of tracks, where you turn left

towards the mature beech woods which crown Gallow Hill Ⓓ. Once you are in the woodland, take the path to the left, which takes you up the side of the plantation. From the northern part of the wood you may be able to see Gardenholm Linn Ⓔ in the distance to the left.

▶4 At the northern end of the wood, look for a small path to the left, through the conifers. This is about 50 paces before the track narrows into a single-file footpath. On reaching a field, bear right to walk through the precincts of Archbank Farm.

▶5 Turn left at the main road up to Moffat Well Ⓕ. Retrace your steps to where you emerged from the farm. Turn left and follow the unclassified road for ½ mile (800m) back towards Moffat.

▶6 Turn right onto Selkirk Road, then right again to reach the High Street. Turn left and retrace your steps back to Station Park.

---

revolutionized the construction of roads, is buried. The cemetery is also the last resting place of many Covenanting refugees who died for their religious beliefs during the 'killing times' in the 17th century.

Further up the street stands the Ram Statue Ⓒ, a reminder of Moffat's past role as a centre for sheep farming. It was given to the town in 1875 as a watering place for travellers and animals. Local legend has it that the sculptor, William Brodie, committed suicide when he realized that he had made the ram without any ears.

Across the road is the town hall, formerly the baths and pump room. The building had an assembly hall and reading rooms and was the venue for promenade concerts, art exhibitions and balls. The Grand

September Ball was an important event in the district's social calendar. Next door is the splendid Moffat House Hotel, designed by one of the eminent Adam family.

Gallow Hill Ⓓ, a pleasant knoll to the north of Moffat, is crowned by a beech wood. As the name suggests, it was once the site of executions. On the Moffat side is Beechgrove, venue of the South of Scotland Lawn Tennis Championships, which

▶ *The road to Moffat Well in Birnock Glen. The discovery of the well by the bishop's daughter heralded the town's prosperity as an inland spa.*

predate Wimbledon.

Away to the north-west of the town is Gardenholm Linn Ⓔ, a beauty spot where the remains of one of the victims of Dr Buck Ruxton, a Lancastrian murderer of the 1930s, were found. Golden eagles have been known to feed in the Moffat hills in recent years. The hills ring to the cries of feral goats and the cawing of ravens, and you may see them as you head towards Moffat Well Ⓕ.

MARJORIE O' THE MONIE LOCHS

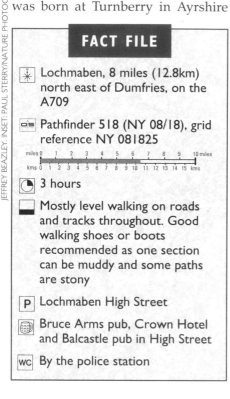

JEFFREY BEAZLEY. INSET: PAUL STERRY/NATURE PHOTOGRAPHERS

▲*The ruins of the 13th-century Lochmaben Castle now stand on a peninsula overlooking Castle Loch. Cowbane (inset), found around the lochs, is often fatal to cattle.*

Exploring the streets and waters of a historic Annandale town

The valley of Annandale in south-west Scotland is gently rolling pastoral country, very different from the rugged landscapes further north. There are many attractive towns and villages in the area, though none perhaps as charming as the royal burgh of Lochmaben, which stood on the old main road that linked England and Scotland in the Middle Ages.

Lochmaben has five lochs surrounding it. There used to be seven,

but the Grummel Loch, once used for ducking witches, and the Broomhill Loch were drained long ago. This caused Robert Burns to dub it 'Marjorie o' the Monie Lochs'. Burns frequently visited Lochmaben and, though he criticised the burghers for their liking of whisky, he wrote lovingly of the place and its people and was made a Freeman of the Burgh. The minister's daughter was the inspiration for his poem, *The Blue-Eyed Lassie*.

The local people are also proud of the town's connection with another Scottish hero, Robert the Bruce. There is a street and a pub named after the Bruce family. There is a tradition that Robert the Bruce was born in the town of Lochmaben, although it is also claimed that he was born at Turnberry in Ayrshire

FACT FILE

- ✳ Lochmaben, 8 miles (12.8km) north east of Dumfries, on the A709
- ⓄⓈ Pathfinder 518 (NY 08/18), grid reference NY 081825

  miles 0 1 2 3 4 5 6 7 8 9 10 miles
  kms 0 1 2 3 4 5 6 7 8 9 10 11 12 13 14 15 kms

- ◔ 3 hours
- ▭ Mostly level walking on roads and tracks throughout. Good walking shoes or boots recommended as one section can be muddy and some paths are stony
- 🅿 Lochmaben High Street
- 🍺 Bruce Arms pub, Crown Hotel and Balcastle pub in High Street
- 🚾 By the police station

▼*The Mill Loch is home to various waterbirds and to the bream, an uncommon fish in northern waters.*

JEFFREY BEAZLEY

THE WALK

LOCHMABEN

The start of the walk is by the statue of Robert the Bruce Ⓐ in Lochmaben.

1 Proceed to the right of the town hall, and follow the main road until it passes the end of Mill Loch Ⓑ. Turn left into a side road between houses, with the loch to your left.

2 Just before an old railway bridge, turn left down a small track signposted as a public right-of-way. This leads to the loch. Follow the path that runs along the side of the loch, until you reach a gate. Woodycastle Ⓒ is over to your right.

3 Go through the gate and follow a signposted right-of-way the length of a narrow field. Go through

the gate by a group of houses. Follow a cattle track along the front of the houses, shortly bearing to the right. Continue for 220 yards (200m).

4 Turn sharp left up a rough gravel track. The track joins an unclassified road to the south of Watchill. Turn left.

5 Turn left on the A709. After ¼ mile (400m), turn sharp right down a by-road. Turn first left to Lochmaben Cemetery.

6 Turn left immediately after the cemetery. Cross the Vendace Burn, with Kirk Loch Ⓓ on your left, and emerge next to Castlehill Farm.

7 Turn left, and follow the lane to the motte Ⓔ and to Castle Hill Ⓕ. Retrace your steps past the farmyard to a gate. Cross and take the right of way along the field edge to come to the B7020.

8 Turn right, then first left to visit Lochmaben Castle Ⓖ beside Castle Loch. Retrace your steps and continue on the B7020 to the junction by Lochmaben's church. Turn left along the High Street to return to the start.

◄From Watchill, passed en route, there are fine views of the gently rolling countryside of the Annandale valley.

---

and Guisborough in Yorkshire. What is certain is that the Bruces had their seat at Lochmaben for over a century, and that Robert the Bruce's grandfather died in the town.

The walk starts by the statue to King Robert the Bruce Ⓐ at the northern end of the High Street. In the town hall opposite, a glass jar contains a preserved specimen of the fish for which Lochmaben used to be celebrated; the Lochmaben

vendace. Vendace were found nowhere else in the world apart from Mill Loch Ⓑ and Castle Loch, passed at a later stage of the walk.

FISHY TALE

Local legend has it that the vendace was introduced either by Mary, Queen of Scots or by Robert the Bruce, although zoologists say it swam into the Lochmaben area and became landlocked by the Ice Ages.

The fish was considered a gourmet's delight, although King James VI thought he was being poisoned when he was offered a dish of them at a banquet in Dumfries. An aristocratic club was formed last century to fish for vendace. Later, a working men's club was established, and the Vendace Fishing became a public holiday.

RARE INSECTS

The fish is officially extinct in the Castle Loch, although experts believe there is a chance that the Mill Loch still supports them. The Mill Loch is a Site of Special Scientific Interest, and its edges support some rare plants, including cowbane and marsh stitchwort. There are also two rare species of crane-fly and a rare type of beetle.

The loch is also thought to be the only place north of the border where bream thrive, and they have done so for centuries. In 1305, a servant earned himself half a merk (13⅓d sterling) for travelling from Carlisle to Lochmaben to catch bream for the king. Nowadays, many coarse fishermen travel north from the Midlands to fish the lochs of Lochmaben, there being no close season here.

ROMAN ROAD

To the north of the Mill Loch, there once ran a Roman road. Although no trace remains, it supposedly took a similar route to the old Lockerbie to Dumfries railway line, which closed in 1965. Beyond the line is

▶ *Robert the Bruce's forefathers built a motte and bailey on this site, now part of the local golf course. Lochmaben's second castle (below) was once a powerful island fortress, standing impregnably in Castle Loch (above).*

Woodycastle **G**, the remains of an Iron Age hill fort. It is 212 feet (63m) in diameter, and surrounded by a rampart of earth and stone. There is a tradition that it is the burial-place of several warriors killed in a 9th-century battle. A huge boulder supposedly marks the spot where King Constantine was slain in AD870. Another fanciful legend has it that there is a massive crock of gold buried beneath the boulder.

BESIDE THE LOCH

The walk skirts Kirk Loch **D**, by the side of which there was a prehistoric settlement. In the Middle Ages, there was a church at the head of the loch, from which its name derives. When winters were generally colder,

ALL PHOTOS JEFFREY BEAZLEY

this was a curler's paradise, and home curling internationals were played here last century.

A short diversion takes you to Castle Hill **F**, where you can take in some typical Annandale scenery. To the north are the Lowther Hills, while to the east is Burnswark, a flat-topped, extinct volcano, once the site of a Roman camp. To the west, the conical peak of Criffel dominates the distance.

AN IMPRESSIVE SITE

A visit to the site of the Bruces' castle **E** will leave you in no doubt that it was not Lochmaben's beauty but its strategic location, overlooking a wide swathe of Dumfriesshire, that made it attractive to Robert the Bruce's forefathers, who had two castles in the town.

The first, on this spot, was a typical Norman motte and bailey, with an orchard that stretched down to the loch. The castle was captured by

▲The Jardine monument in Lochmaben's cemetery commemorates the locally-born surgeon who became one of the founders of Hong Kong.

Edward I, and recaptured by William Wallace. Now long-since abandoned, its motte has been put to use by the local golf course; it is currently one of the tees, so watch out for flying golf balls if you want to take a closer look at the motte.

About ¾ mile (1.2km) to the south is the second castle ❻. This was actually built by Edward I on what used to be an island in what is now called the Castle Loch. The water level was lowered when the outlet burn was dredged, so that it now stands on a peninsula. The castle was captured by Robert the Bruce and an Anglo-Scottish treaty was signed there in 1323. It was later captured and recaptured, besieged and liberated, and saw its fair share of border history. It was once the most powerful fortress in the region, but it is now in glorious ruins, given over to ivy and picnickers.

GEESE AND GOOSANDERS

Castle Loch is well-known for its birdlife, and is run by the local council as a nature reserve. Like the Mill Loch, it is a Site of Special Scientific Interest. In winter, geese arrive in their thousands and roost by the loch, which is surrounded by alder and willows. The loch supports more than one per cent of the British wintering population of goosanders. Great crested grebes also find sanctuary here, and you may be lucky enough to see the odd shelduck or pochard, which breed somewhat elusively in the neighbourhood. Mute swans, coots and moorhens are more easily seen. There used to be crannogs (fortified dwellings built on artificial islands of boulders) on the loch in prehistoric times; in fact, in dry weather, the remains of one can sometimes be seen protruding above the water.

HEADING HOME

The road back to Lochmaben goes along the lochside, although it is difficult to get a view of the waters unless you make a diversion through the strip of trees between the road and the loch. As you enter the town, you pass Lochmaben's church, which was built in 1819.

From the left side of the High street, just opposite Bruce's statue, you may like to visit the old cemetery, which has some interesting monuments. One of them commemorates Dr. William Jardine, the Lochmaben-born ship's surgeon who was one of the founders of the colony of Hong Kong, and whose life-story was the inspiration behind James Clavell's novel, *Tai Pan*.

Robert the Bruce

A key figure in the history of medieval Scotland, Robert the Bruce was descended from Robert de Brus, a Norman knight who had been given the Vale of Annan by King David in the 12th century. The influential Scotsman could also claim King David as a forebear through the female line.

When Alexander III died without a son in 1286, Edward I of England intervened in the crisis of succession, initially by invitation. He effectively took over in 1291. Robert the Bruce, born in 1274, first came to prominence in William Wallace's rebellion of 1297. Following the English victory at Falkirk, Bruce became the leader of the struggle.

He was crowned king at Scone in March 1306, but fled to Ulster following several defeats in battle. After Edward I died in 1307, Bruce

returned to Scotland to fight a guerilla war against the English.

In 1314, a large English army, said by some to be 100,000, but more likely a quarter that size, went north under Edward II to finally destroy Bruce. At Bannockburn, they were routed by the Scots, whom they outnumbered by at least 2 to 1.

Bruce died in 1329, and in 1371 was succeeded by Robert II, son of Bruce's daughter and Walter the Steward. He founded the royal house of Stuart, which ruled an independent Scotland until the Act of Union of 1603, when the Stuarts took over the throne of a united England and Scotland.

This manuscript illustration, dated 1306, shows Robert the Bruce with his second wife, Elizabeth; their son succeeded to the Scottish throne as David II.

JASON SMALLEY. INSET: DON SMITH/NATURE PHOTOGRAPHERS

◄*The view back along the cliffs from Gallie Craig to the lighthouse where the walk starts. The dorsal fin of the basking shark (above) can sometimes be seen cleaving the offshore waters.*

from the watery depths, foretelling the imminent death of any descendant of the McCullochs of Myrton.

According to local legend, one such episode occurred many years ago on the Feast of Lammas (the first day of August and traditionally the beginning of the harvest). A young McCulloch was wagered he would not venture past the haunted hawthorn to Kirkmaiden Church. He left the inn, bible in hand, and later that night the bell was heard to ring out across the parish. Next morning, he was found impaled on the hawthorn, his heart torn from his breast. In commemoration, the hawthorn earned the title 'Man

Around steep cliffs at Scotland's southernmost tip

The Mull of Galloway has one of the most rugged and dramatic shorelines in the country, and lies between the deep blue waters of Luce Bay and the Irish Channel. The Mull has always been remote. A place of strange beliefs and customs, its history is as rich and colourful as the countless wild flowers that

carpet the jagged clifftops.

The walk begins at the lighthouse **A** on the tip of the Mull, 269 feet (82m) above the thundering seas. Shipwrecks were common on this treacherous coast until the 60-foot (18-m) lighthouse was built in 1828 and its piercing foghorn echoed out across Luce Bay.

From here, another unearthly sound has supposedly been heard — the toll of a ghostly bell. Lost beneath the waves while on its way to Kirkmaiden Church in a rowing boat, it is said periodically to ring

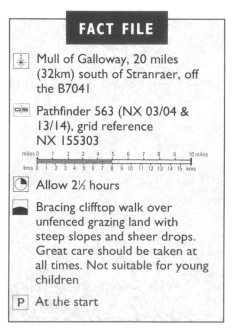

FACT FILE

✳ Mull of Galloway, 20 miles (32km) south of Stranraer, off the B7041

🖵 Pathfinder 563 (NX 03/04 & 13/14), grid reference NX 155303

miles 0 1 2 3 4 5 6 7 8 9 10 miles
kms 0 1 2 3 4 5 6 7 8 9 10 11 12 13 14 15 kms

◔ Allow 2½ hours

▬ Bracing clifftop walk over unfenced grazing land with steep slopes and sheer drops. Great care should be taken at all times. Not suitable for young children

Ⓟ At the start

THE WALK

MULL OF GALLOWAY

The walk begins from the car park by the Mull of Galloway lighthouse.

1 Go through the gate into the grounds of the lighthouse **A**. Follow the tarmac road, but when it bends right, continue on a grassy path in the direction of the lighthouse.

2 Before the lighthouse, bear left towards a pole, then continue ahead to Lagvag Point **B**, passing between a white building on your left and the lighthouse on your right. (This involves a descent down a steep, grassy slope and should not be attempted if the grass is wet.) Retrace your steps towards the car park, but turn left to follow the wall to the clifftop. Turn right along the cliffs and follow them until you are above West Tarbet **C**.

3 Bear right along the top of the hill above the bay to a tarmac road. Turn left, and just before a cattle grid, turn right alongside a wire fence past the Bay of East Tarbet **D**. Cut diagonally left across the field to a stone wall.

4 Follow the line of the wall, climbing a stone step stile to cross the wire fence. Bear left and continue to follow the stone wall along the cliff tops. At the end of the wall, follow the wire fence until the going gets boggy above St Medan's Cave **E** and Chapel Wells, then retrace your steps to the cattle grid and turn left.

5 Take the next turning left down the track, just before the Double Dykes **F**, towards East Tarbet. Bear right to pass between some buildings. Just beyond them, turn right to follow a sheep path above the shore. (Care is needed along this slope.)

6 After about ½ mile (800m), bear right up to the crest of the hill. Continue across the pasture to the road. Turn left and follow the road back to the car park.

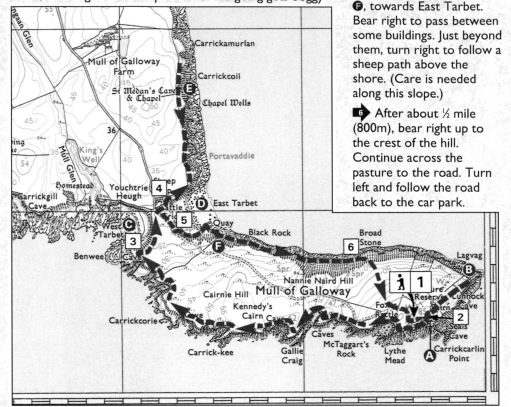

Wrap', a name still used by locals until the early 1900s.

Walking towards Lagvag Point **B**, the view is awe-inspiring. It used to be said that you could see seven kingdoms from the headland; Scotland, Ireland, England, Wales, the Isle of Man, Strathclyde and Heaven. The narrow cliff ledges and crevices are crowded with raucous herring gulls, great and lesser black-backed gulls, shags, razorbills, black guillemots and fulmars, which dive and wheel endlessly, twisting in the wind and soaring high above the sheer rock faces.

At nesting time, guillemots use the narrowest, most exposed cliff ledges, safe from four-legged predators. Higher still, kittiwakes build nests of seaweed cemented with mud and coated with droppings.

While colonies may overlap, each species' individual preferences help avoid too much squabbling.

A century ago, almost the only British colony of fulmars was on St Kilda. The birds' rapid spread since then is attributed to modern fishing methods, where offal is thrown overboard at sea. They now haunt the perpendicular cliffs of the Mull throughout most of the year, but close contact is inadvisable as they have a habit of repelling intruders with a foul jet of stomach oil.

COLOURFUL CLIFFTOPS

Westward along the clifftops, the high ledges are a blaze of colour, with dainty sea pinks, mountain milk-vetch, yellow vetch and the pretty star-like flower of spring squill. Years ago, locals scrambled down the dangerous cliff-face in

◄*The walk starts from the Mull of Galloway lighthouse, built in 1828. Ever since, the lighthouse has been a vital landmark to ships passing between the Mull and the Isle of Man.*

JASON SMALLEY

ALL PHOTOS: JASON SMALLEY

Nature Walk

THE GUILLEMOT breeds on sheer cliffs around Britain. Its white breast and dark head are clearly visible in flight. Wing beats are rapid and the flight fast and low over the water.

THE EGGS vary in colour, with a base colour of white through shades of brown, cream, blue or green. All are pear-shaped, which stops them rolling off the narrow nesting ledges.

MIKE WOODS

▲ *The natural bay at West Tarbet (above) and the sheltered harbour at East Tarbet lie on either side of a narrow neck of land (above left).*

search of rock samphire, rare in these parts, which can be pickled or boiled and eaten with butter — hence it is sometimes known as 'sea asparagus'. In summer, common blue butterflies lay their eggs on bird's-foot trefoil, while the meadow brown, with its dark eye-spots, lays eggs on the heathy grasses.

CROWDED WATERS

Far beneath, seals are sometimes seen bobbing and diving in the off-shore waters. The Mull's cold, deep currents are excellent fishing grounds; record catches of skate, ling, flounder, turbot and dogfish have been made, not to mention 80-pound (36-kg) conger eels and four basking sharks. The latter were taken in one day between the Mull and the Isle of Man, and weighed a total of 13 tons.

The route continues to East and West Tarbet on either side of a narrow isthmus. Until the 19th century, fishing boats were dragged across from bay to bay to avoid the fierce current at the tip of the Mull.

The perilous coast beyond West Tarbet **C** was once used as a landing point for smugglers bringing cargoes from the Isle of Man. Many Galloway farms had secret underground passages to the shore.

▶ *The coastline along the entire length of the walk is a rugged one of cliffs, rocks and occasional shingle beaches.*

Queen Victoria and Prince Albert anchored their yacht off the quieter bay of East Tarbet **D** during a royal cruise. The Prince Consort set off to climb to the lighthouse, but was defeated by a heavy squall of rain.

As you head north along the clifftops, you reach a point where St Medan's Cave **E** lies below you. A few pathetic ruins, hidden in the craggy rock face, are all that remain of a chapel. The original path down the cliff, now virtually crumbled away, is hard to find and very dangerous. In 1872, the Marquess of Bute organized an evacuation here that yielded pilgrim badges, brass mountings and a beautiful sandstone statue of the Virgin Mary, or possibly St Medan herself. Unfortunately, because the Marquess had recently converted to Catholicism, an enraged anti-Catholic mob from Stranraer demonstrated their piety by flinging the treasures into the sea.

St Medan, after whom the nearby parish of Kirkmaiden is named, was an Irish princess who fled her own

The Galloway Cannibal

CHARLES GRANT

JASON SMALLEY

This gruesome waxwork in an Edinburgh museum depicts Beane and his wife roasting human limbs over an open fire.

14 children and incestuously produced 31 grandchildren. The family supported itself by pouncing on travellers, robbing and murdering them, and carrying their bodies back to the cave, where they were pickled in sea water or smoke-cured and then eaten.

More than 1,000 men, women and children disappeared without trace. Severed arms and legs were washed up on the lonely shores of Galloway, and supernatural tales evolved to explain what was happening. Several innocent people were found guilty of murder on circumstantial evidence and hanged. The population of the region began to shrink.

Eventually, a man escaped an attack to tell the tale of how a savage band had torn his wife to pieces. King James I led an army of 400 men into Galloway.

Bloodhounds discovered the family's hiding place in a labyrinth of caverns. Captured and taken to Leith, every member of the family was summarily executed, even the babies. The males were mutilated and left to bleed to death, while the females were burned alive.

▲ These mounded Iron Age earthworks, the Double Dykes, are visible on the clifftop near East Tarbet.

and been one of the largest Iron Age strongholds in Britain.

It was here, reputedly, that the last four members of the Pictish race, a father and his three sons, were finally conquered by the Scots. For seven days they defended themselves from the embankment, sustained by their supply of 'Biadh-nan-treun', the food of heroes.

SECRET POTION

As the food ran out, they began to weaken, and they were forced to strike a bargain — if the Scots would spare the life of Trost, the eldest son, and thus preserve the race, Trost would disclose the Picts' secret formula for heather ale.

The father and two other sons could not bear to see this happen, and crossed the dykes to their deaths. Rather than betray his tribe, Trost grabbed the Scots' emissary, a Pictish traitor, and leapt from the cliffs shouting 'The secret is saved'. Both men died, and with them was lost the secret recipe for heather ale, a wonderful brew made from sweet-scented purple heather.

The Mull of Galloway is associated with the legend of Sawney Beane, a murderer whose bloody story was first written down in the 17th century. There are enough details for the tale to be based in fact, but authorities cannot agree as to dates (the range of disagreement spans nearly two centuries) or places.

Perhaps the most authentic version is that Beane was born near Edinburgh in around 1400 and worked as a hedger and ditcher. When still a young man, he ran off with a girlfriend and set up home in a cave on the Galloway coast.

Over the next 25 years, they had

country to escape the attentions of an over-amorous suitor. The story goes that before leaving, she plucked out her eyes and threw them at his feet. She crossed the Irish Sea on a floating rock, and her sight was miraculously restored when she bathed herself in the waters of Chapel Wells, three natural rock basins in the cliff-face that fill with seawater at high tide. Thus, in later years, the waters were supposed to have great healing powers.

On the way back to East Tarbet, huge ramparts are evident beneath the grassy banks of the Mull, stretching right across this strip of land. There is evidence of a hut circle at the south-west end of the ramparts. These Double Dykes ❻ were probably the bastion of a huge fort that may have covered the entire Mull

▼ From a point above St Medan's Cave and Chapel there are views all the way back down the Mull to the lighthouse.

JASON SMALLEY

THE EILDON HILLS

MORRISON/EDINBURGH PHOTOGRAPHIC LIBRARY   INSET: JOHN HAYWARD/NHPA

An exploration around Sir Walter Scott's country

This walk involves a gentle hill climb to the summit of the Eildon Hills, the most prominent viewpoint in the central part of the Tweed Valley. There are good views of Melrose and the Tweed as you climb the hills and from the summit

BORDERS REGIONAL COUNCIL

FACT FILE

* Melrose, 4 miles (6km) southeast of Galashiels, just off the A7

* Pathfinder 461 (NT 43/53), grid reference NT 547339

miles 0 1 2 3 4 5 6 7 8 9 10 miles
kms 0 1 2 3 4 5 6 7 8 9 10 11 12 13 14 15 kms

* Allow 3 hours

* A steady, straightforward climb. Well-marked grassy footpaths through fields and moorland. After heavy rain, path is very muddy from stage **7** onwards

* **P** In the centre of Melrose opposite the entrance to the abbey

* Hotels, cafés, shops at Melrose

there is a superb panorama on a clear day. The return journey leads around the slopes of the hill with constantly changing views of the surrounding countryside.

The triple peaks of the heather-

▲ *The splendid view over the Eildon Hills and the River Tweed has changed little since Sir Walter Scott lived here. (inset) The large-flowered butterwort. (below left) Rooftops of Melrose.*

clad Eildon Hills, known to the Romans as 'Trimontium', dominate Melrose and the Tweed valley. According to legend they were once a single cone. The hill was supposedly split in three by a demon belonging to the medieval wizard Michael Scott. Geologists prefer a more prosaic explanation: the hills are the remains of a mass of volcanic lava which intruded into the surrounding sandstone underground and is exposed at the surface as the result of millions of years of erosion.

LEGENDS GALORE

The Eildons are steeped in Border legend. A stone beside the A6091 to the east marks the site of the Eildon Tree under which the medieval poet Thomas of Ercildoun (Earlston, near Melrose) is said to have met with the Queen of Elfland and to have been

THE WALK

MELROSE - THE TOP OF THE EILDON HILLS

The walk begins at the car park opposite the entrance to Melrose Abbey **A**.

1 From the car park walk into the market place of Melrose. Go through the market place, past the mercat cross **B** and follow the B6359 road to the south, uphill, under the by-pass.

2 About 20 yards (18 metres) beyond the by-pass turn left down steps through a gap between two houses, following a sign marked 'Eildon Walk'.

3 Follow the footpath which leads straight uphill along the edge of two fields and over stiles until you reach open moorland.

4 The path now slants uphill to your right making for the saddle between the two main summits of the Eildon Hills, with the old quarry of Bourjo **C** further to your right.

5 From the saddle turn left along the well-marked footpath which leads through the ramparts of the hillfort **D** to the top of Eildon Hill North. From the summit, with its traces of the Roman signal station **E**, retrace your steps to the saddle.

6 If time and energy permit, you may also like to follow the footpath which leads in the opposite direction to the slightly higher summit of Eildon Mid Hill with its prehistoric burial cairn **F**.

7 From the saddle follow a footpath which leads to the south along the right-hand side of a shallow valley until you reach the edge of a belt of woodland. Turn left and follow the track which runs along the edge of the plantations.

8 Just beyond the steepest part of the hillside above you the track forks. Follow the left-hand branch slightly uphill around the slope of the hill and then downhill for a short stretch, looking towards the site of the Roman fort of Newstead.

9 The path leads down to the end of a long thin belt of woodland. A short distance beyond the start of the trees a footpath leads off to the left, contouring the northern slopes of the hill until it joins the path that you took on your outward journey.

10 Retrace your steps to Melrose.

MORRISON/EDINBURGH PHOTOGRAPHIC LIBRARY

carried off to her country for seven years. The hills are also associated with King Arthur who, with his knights, is supposed to lie sleeping in a cave beneath them.

The walk starts opposite the entrance to Melrose Abbey **A**, the greatest of the Border abbeys, the ruins of which are still impressive. As well as lying at the heart of the romantic Scott country, the abbey church is the last resting place for

In spite of its destruction in several cross-border raids, the ruins of Melrose Abbey are a stately reminder of its former wealth and glory.

the heart of Robert the Bruce.

The abbey was founded in 1136 by Cistercian monks from Rievaulx in Yorkshire. King David I granted the monks thousands of acres of land in the area around the monastery. They also acquired extensive grazing rights in more distant hill areas and built up a flock of around 12,500 sheep, making Melrose the richest of the Border abbeys.

MELROSE ABBEY

The original 12th-century church, parts of which survive at the western end of the present building, was plain and austere. It was badly damaged by English attacks during the 14th century and after the last devastating attack in 1385, a major rebuilding of the church was undertaken. Work continued through the 15th century under the direction of master masons from Yorkshire and France. The new church was built in an exuberant and ornate style, with a wealth of delicate tracery and fine sculpture. The church was badly damaged by the English in 1544 and 1545, while many of the statues were probably defaced at the time of the Reformation. Although part of the nave continued to be used as a church until the 19th century, the abbey was neglected and rapidly fell into ruin.

DAYLIGHT ROBBERY

The cloisters and the surrounding buildings stood to the north of the church, instead of in the usual position to the south. This made it easier for the monks to lay on a water supply via a 1 1/4 mile (2 km) long canal from the Tweed, which can still be seen beside the abbey.

Most of the domestic buildings around the cloisters were robbed to their foundations after the Reformation, although their outlines can still be traced. The detached house

▲ *Eildon Mid Hill and Bourjo quarry - a long haul for monks rebuilding the abbey. (right) Casting a fly in the Tweed in the shadow of the bridges.*

to the north of the abbey appears originally to have been the abbot's residence. It was remodelled around 1590 for the lay commendator who took charge of the abbey and its lands after the Reformation.

Enough remains of the eastern end of the church to show how magnificent it must have looked. The abbey is open to the public and is a

fascinating place to visit. Among the curious gargoyles, look for one of a pig playing a set of bagpipes!

The walk continues through the market place of Melrose **B** with its 16th-century mercat cross. The town grew up at the gates of the abbey as a market centre belonging to the monks. Halfway up the climb to the saddle between Eildon Hill North and Eildon Mid Hill you can see on your right the remains of an old quarry with the quaint name of Bourjo **C**. This was where stone for the rebuilt 15th-century abbey was quarried, although the monks may also have taken stone from the nearby Roman fort. Traces of a road for the sleds which transported the stone can be seen running down from the quarry towards the abbey.

ROMAN RUIN

As you make the final climb to the summit of Eildon Hill North you pass through the ramparts of an Iron Age hillfort **D**. The fort was a major tribal capital, belonging to a people known as the Selgovae.

It started as a small fort on the top of the hill and was later extended. The three lines of ramparts from the final phase of construction have a circuit of over a mile (1.6km) and enclose some 40 acres (20 hectares). In many places they appear as terraces rather than as upstanding features — the ramparts were deliberately demolished by the Romans.

The Selgovae appear to have been a warlike tribe and once the Romans had subdued them they made them

Abbotsford lies in a magical setting and is still lived in by the direct descendants of Sir Walter Scott.

abandon their fort which they then demolished. They then consolidated their hold on the area by establishing a major base at the foot of the Eildon Hills.

Inside the ramparts of the hillfort there are traces of hut platforms scooped into the hillside. Nearly 300 have been identified; if only a proportion of these were permanently occupied the fort must have had a population of over 1,000.

On the summit of Eildon Hill North are the remains of a circular ditch which once enclosed a Roman signal station **E**. From it, messages could be relayed to and from the fort below, as well as to other outposts in the area. From the summit there is a superb view over Melrose and its surrounding villages, most of which originated as monastic farms.

Downstream from Melrose the

Sir Walter Scott

Sir Walter Scott (1771-1832) is closely associated with the Eildon Hills. As a boy suffering from the after-effects of polio, he was sent to Sandyknowes farm, just across the River Tweed to the east, to recuperate. Local stories, including tales of the supernatural and the exploits of the Border reivers in war, feud and foray, fired his imagination.

A portrait of Sir Walter Scott by his contemporary, Edwin Landseer.

NATIONAL PORTRAIT GALLERY

His first major epic poem, *The Lay of the Last Minstrel*, which established him as a literary figure before he turned to writing novels, was set around the Eildon Hills. Although the supernatural elements in the poem and the over-chivalrous picture of Border society may seem unconvincing today, it contains some fine descriptive passages, notably one on the ruins of Melrose Abbey viewed by moonlight.

In 1812, he bought the farm of Cartleyhole, 3 miles (4.8km) west of Melrose. Renaming it 'Abbotsford', Scott began a major programme of rebuilding which was not completed until 1822. He demolished the farm buildings and created a Gothic-style mansion which was a Romantic extravaganza on a small scale, incorporating in its masonry features collected from a variety of historic sites in the Lothians and the Borders. Here he wrote many of his novels and housed his superb collection of historical relics.

Scott died at Abbotsford in

Abbotsford lies in a magical setting and is still lived in by the direct descendants of Sir Walter Scott.

BY KIND PERMISSION OF MRS MAXWELL SCOTT, ABBOTSFORD

1832 and was buried in Dryburgh Abbey, a short distance downstream from Melrose. The road to the abbey runs high above the river with a magnificent panorama of the Eildon Hills, supposedly the writer's favourite view. As his body was carried along this road, his carriage horses, pulling the hearse, stopped here out of habit. Today an indicator plaque at Scott's View picks out the various landmarks.

---

valley of the Tweed narrows. Here the Roman Dere Street crossed the river. Today there are three bridges; the 18th-century road bridge, its modern replacement and a graceful 19th-century railway viaduct. To the south other prominent hills stand out, including Dunion, Minto Crags and Rubers Law. These hills mark the sites of former volcanoes whose cones have been completely eroded. All that remains are the hard plugs of lava which once plugged the vents in the bottom of

their craters. Beyond these isolated hills runs the long blue line of the Cheviots. To the north lie the Moorfoots and Lammermuirs and to the west are the Tweeddale Hills, with the Galloway Hills sometimes visible far to the south-west.

Close to the summit of Eildon Mid Hill is a prominent prehistoric burial cairn **❻**. As you come round the eastern side of Eildon Hill North there is a good view over the site of the Roman fort at Newstead. Nothing is visible now of this important Roman base. Unlike the native Britons, the Romans generally built their forts on low ground, trusting to the quality of their defences and the superior discipline of their troops rather than to inaccessibility. As a result Newstead, in common with many other Roman sites, has been levelled by centuries of weather and cultivation.

The plan of the fort has been recovered by excavation. There were four successive forts on the

JOHN WATNEY

The old railway station at Melrose is now a source of local information.

same site, the last one having a stone wall 6 feet (2 metres) thick, backed by a clay rampart 46 feet (14 metres) wide with ditches in front.

CURIOUS DESIGN

The old railway station, a grade A listed building designed like a Jacobean country house and dating from 1849, stands beside the by-pass. It has been converted into a craft shop, art gallery and restaurant. It also houses an exhibition relating to the Roman occupation of southern Scotland and the nearby fort of Newstead, and another about the Waverley Route, the former railway line from Edinburgh to Carlisle through the Borders. The line, which was named after the Waverley novels of Sir Walter Scott, was closed in 1969. Melrose also has a motor museum in Annay Road just beyond the abbey. Sir Walter Scott's former home, Abbotsford, which he re-named because the land had once belonged to the Abbot of Melrose, is off the road to Galashiels 3 miles (4.8km) to the west. It is open to the public and worth visiting.

MARCHING THROUGH COLDSTREAM

GLYN SATTERLEY. INSET: ROGER TIDMAND/NHPA

A town and country walk through the home of the guards

Coldstream, as the town song proclaims, is 'The first true Border Toon'. The River Tweed forms the Border and the English county of Northumbria is but a stone's throw away.

The town, which has a population of less than 2,000, is much better known than other comparable small towns thanks to its association with the 2nd Regiment of Foot Guards.

Though Coldstream is close to the English border, there is less evidence here in 'The Merse' or Eastern

FACT FILE

* ☀ On A697/A698 immediately upon crossing the border at Coldstream Bridge

* ▱ Pathfinders 451 (NT 84/94) and 463 (NT 83/93), grid reference NT 843398

miles 0 1 2 3 4 5 6 7 8 9 10 miles
kms 0 1 2 3 4 5 6 7 8 9 10 11 12 13 14 15 kms

* ◔ Allow 3½ hours to include museum

* ▭ Easy town and country walk. No steep gradients but one possible muddy section in wet weather

* P Henderson Park, Market Square, Leet Bridge and Court House Place off High Street

* ⛾ Hotels, pubs, and a café

* WC Abbey Road and Court House Place

* ⊞ Museum open Easter to end of October, Monday-Saturday 10-1pm, 2-5pm, Sunday 2-5pm

▲ *The River Tweed meanders as it reaches the town of Coldstream. Sand martins (left) are members of the swallow family. They scrape long tunnels in sand banks for nests.*

March, of casual cattle stealing and downright theft than there was in other places. 'Reiving' as this kind of stealing was called, was a way of life further west, especially around Teviodale, although 'The Merse' was subject to organized punitive invasions by English forces.

▼ *The Marriage House once had a reputation for clandestine weddings.*

GLYN SATTERLEY

Prior to the reorganization of local government, Coldstream was a Police Burgh with the full dignity of provost and town council. Unlike many border towns Coldstream has never had an involvement in the wool industry. It owed its early existence to the fact that it was a convenient fording place on the River Tweed. The Tweed is usually a calm river under summer skies, but in August 1948 it rose to such a height that canoes were paddled in Market Place.

ROMAN SOLDIERS

Little is known of the town's early history although at one time primary school teachers were wont to tell pupils that Caestrum is Latin for Coldstream, the name being given by Roman soldiers who found the

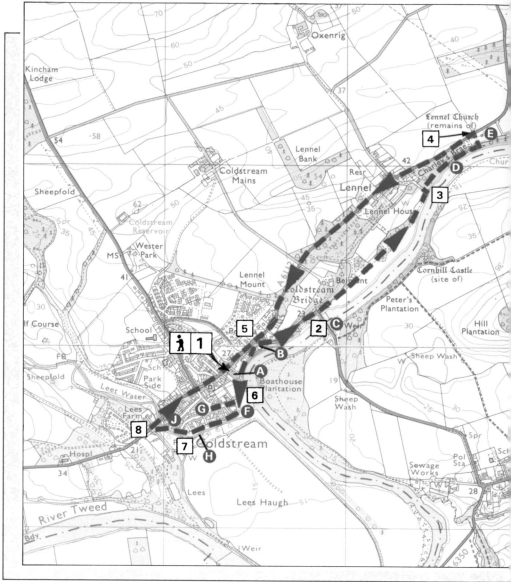

▲ *The walk leads into the countryside through woodland. Coldstream bridge (below) was designed by George Smeaton and built in 1766. At the centre, it is possible to stand with one foot in England and one in Scotland.*

bitterly cold waters of the Tweed uncomfortable.

As a main fording place, even although not on any of the main routes used by the Legions, it is most likely that Romans did pass this way. Evidence is provided by the signal station and marching camp which were established a few miles north of the town. As to whether the local name has any association with these occupying forces we can only guess.

Of the convent founded in 1165 by Gospatrick, Earl of Dunbar, only the place names of Penitents Walk, Nuns Walk and Abbey Road remain. Edward I billeted troops in the Coldstream convent in 1290 and 1296. His troops are said to have caused some damage although the building was not sacked.

Following the Battle of Flodden in 1533, the Prioress of Coldstream is thought to have arranged burial for the bodies of the nobility and high-ranking churchmen who were slain along with King James IV. Flodden itself lies over the Border near the village of Branxton. Where the battle terminated, a Celtic Cross raised on rough-hewn granite blocks is simply dedicated 'To the

THE WALK

COLDSTREAM

The walk starts at Henderson Park adjoining High Street.

1 Leave Henderson Park **A** turning sharp right along the High Street to 'Charlie' as Coldstreamers affectionately call the monument **B**. Continue past the monument on the roadside path towards Coldstream Bridge **C**. From the centre of the Bridge return towards Coldstream. On the upstream side of the bridge, a sign points to the 'Coldstream Country Walk'.

2 Descend the steps beside the sign. Pass under the dry arch ignoring the 'Private' sign ahead which refers to the weir now on your right. Continue for 50 yards (45 metres) passing through a gate, then around two fishermen's huts where a sign points towards the river bank. Pass through a further gate where the well-defined path heads downstream on the right of a two-strand, electrified cattle fence. Continue along this path. Gradually the haugh, as these riverside meadows are known, narrows to a point where a track descends downhill from Lennel Village.

3 Pass through a gate from the riverside, then follow a sign pointing to Lennel for 50 yards (46 metres) up a broad track. At this point, follow a sign pointing right, indicating the Country Walk through Charlie's Brae **D**, into woodland. After going first through woodland of sycamore and other hardwoods, then through a conifer plantation for 330 yards (300 metres), the path emerges to overlook the Tweed with views up and downstream and beyond to the Cheviot Hills. About 50 yards (45 metres) further on, the path enters the old churchyard **E** of Lennel. Keep to the footpath nearest the river, heading towards the ruins of what was once Coldstream's Parish Church.

4 Turn left out of the churchyard onto the A6112 to walk westwards for 1½ miles (2.4 km) through Lennel, back to Coldstream.

5 Turn left at the police station. Cross the road and pass 'Charlie'. Turn right through a gap in the low wall a short distance beyond a wooden summer-house-type building, which marks the start of Nun's walk. As the walk descends to Tweed Green **F** care should be taken as there is no hand rail on the river side. Nun's walk ends in a sharp right-hand bend.

6 Ignore the road to the left, but continue into Market Place where 50 yards (45 metres) along on the right is the Coldstream Guards Museum **G** in Guards House. After visiting the Museum, retrace your steps to Tweed Green (6). Turn right to where the River Leet joins the Tweed. Follow the banks of the River Leet along Penitent's walk and you will arrive at the end of Leet Green **H**.

7 Turn right to cross a wooden footbridge, pass through a picnic area and car park to the west end of the Leet Bridge **J**.

8 Turn right over the bridge and continue along High Street to return to the start at Henderson Park.

Brave of Both Nations'.

Flodden is remembered in Coldstream every August during the town's annual celebrations, including a cavalcade which crosses the Border to commemorate the sad event. Led by the Coldstreamer, a young man elected to carry the town standard for the week, the Flodden cavalcade is marked with an oration by a person of national distinction.

FLOWER GARDENS

Henderson Park **A** is named after a medical family who had long associations with the town. It is a jewel in Coldstream's crown, as Coldstream, again according to the town song, is a 'jewel in Scotia's Croon'. Ablaze with flower gardens from spring right through to autumn, Henderson Park is worth a visit in its own right. A granite plinth overlooks the River Tweed, recording the granting of the Freedom of the Burgh to the Coldstream Guards in 1968.

At the Park entrance on the right-hand side is a special scented herb garden for the visually handicapped, each plant having its name recorded on a plate in both standard and Braille alphabet. A stone commemorates a visit by H M Queen Elizabeth II and the unveiling of the

Nun's walk takes its name from the Cistercian priory, founded by the Earl of Dunbar in 1165, of which there are no physical remains.

The Coldstream Guards

The link between the small Border town of Coldstream and the famous 2nd Regiment of Foot dates back to the winter of 1659, when General Monck spent around three weeks in the town following the death of Oliver Cromwell.

Monck's regiment had its origins at Berwick on Tweed in 1650. The combined Hesilrige's and Fenwick's regiment were known as, 'Colonel Monck's Regiment of Foot' and were part of Cromwell's 'New Model Army'. They engaged in several campaigns including the battle of Dunbar on 3rd September, 1650.

In January 1660, General Monck set out with his regiment for London. On arrival, many soldiers had their feet bound with rags and sacking, the 34-day, mid-winter march having completely worn out their footwear. The Regiment became engaged in quelling the civil disturbance which had arisen after Cromwell's son Richard had declined to be his father's successor.

After the Restoration of Charles II, Monck's Regiment made the symbolic gesture of laying down their arms at Tower Hill, before picking them up in the service of the Crown as the Lord General's Regiment of Foot Guards. It was only after the death of General Monck that the Regiment adopted the name of the 'Coldstream Guards'.

Despite their motto, 'Nulli Secundus' — second to none — 'The Coldstream', as the regiment is known, takes second place in the line to the Grenadier Guards, whose forebears were the personal bodyguards of the deposed Charles while he was in exile.

'The Coldstream' has two claims to fame. It is the oldest Corps by continuous existence, and it is also the only representative by direct descent of the first Regular Army

The Coldstream Guards played a large part in the restoration of Charles II to monarchy when they marched to London in 1660.

raised by Oliver Cromwell as the 'New Model Army'.

The Regiment has maintained close links with Coldstream, including the provision of prizes at the school's annual prize-giving. In August 1968, the links were forged even closer when the Freedom of the Burgh was granted to the Regiment.

▼*A monument in Henderson Park commemorates the Coldstream Guards gaining the Freedom of the Burgh.*

stone by Sir Alec Douglas Home (now Lord Home) of the Hirsel.

Beyond the foothills rise the Cheviots, dominating the southern horizon from which this border range takes its name. At 2,600 feet (815 metres), it is the highest point in the Eastern Borders.

MARRIAGE HOUSE

Downstream the graceful lines of Coldstream Bridge ⒞, designed by engineer George Smeaton, is a tribute to 18th-century design. At the centre of the bridge, there is a bronze plaque on the downstream parapet. The plaque records the building of the bridge between 1763 and 1766, and the strengthening process it underwent in 1960 and 1961. Possibly the mellow, red-tiled

building, known as the Marriage House, on the north end was originally a toll house associated with the bridge. Due to its proximity to the Border, and a difference between English and Scottish marriage laws, it developed something of a reputation as a centre for clandestine marriages. An 1856 Parliamentary Act outlawed such events, but not before one incumbent William Dickson had won a court case brought by the local minister who had challenged the legality of Dickson's 'ministry'.

At Lennel, there is an interesting old churchyard ⒠ in the grounds of what, until 1708, was Coldstream's parish church, though now it stands in ruins. It was here that Scott set *Marmion* on the eve of Flodden.

WHERE SEABIRDS DARE

9

JEFFREY BEAZLEY. INSET: COLIN CARVER/NATURE PHOTOGRAPHERS LTD

Along cliff tops to seabird colonies and a quiet loch

The spectacular cliffs of St Abb's Head provide the setting for an exhilarating walk through one of Britain's most important nesting sites for seabirds. In the summer months, vast colonies of birds congregate here. In 1983, an area of 192 acres (475 hectares) was declared a National Nature Reserve, and the sea beneath the cliffs became a Voluntary Marine Reserve in 1984.

The walk starts from the southern end of the reserve and heads north along the cliff tops. As the path climbs around a bay, there are views of St Abb's Harbour **Ⓐ**, from where a small inshore fishing fleet operates, specializing in lobsters and crabs. There are also boats here that go further out to trawl for prawns.

The cliffs by the harbour are of a different rock from those to the north, and thus so is the flora. This is the only place in the reserve where you will find bracken, for instance, and associated plants like primroses and early purple orchid.

Soon you pass White Heugh **Ⓑ**, a rocky promontory and a foretaste of the dizzying heights and inlets further north. Seabirds gather on the south side of White Heugh; mostly guillemots, with a few razorbills and, at the top of the cliff, grey and white herring gulls. Graceful kittiwakes build their grassy nests in crevices on the vertical cliff faces.

RARE PLANTS

On the steep, ungrazed slope on White Heugh's north side, the rare Scots lovage thrives. Near the path is another rarity, purple milk-vetch. In midsummer, six-spot burnet moths are found here.

Where the path drops down to Burnmouth Harbour, there is a good view of Mire Loch. As you curve round the back of Horsecastle Bay, you can see a submerged forest of

◄ *The type of rock changes as you progress round the walk. These red cliffs are at Starney Bay, St Abb's Head. The guillemot (below left) is one of several seabird species nesting on this coast.*

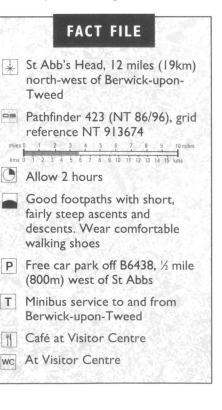

FACT FILE

❋ St Abb's Head, 12 miles (19km) north-west of Berwick-upon-Tweed

⬛ Pathfinder 423 (NT 86/96), grid reference NT 913674

miles 0 1 2 3 4 5 6 7 8 9 10 miles
kms 0 1 2 3 4 5 6 7 8 9 10 11 12 13 14 15 kms

◔ Allow 2 hours

⬤ Good footpaths with short, fairly steep ascents and descents. Wear comfortable walking shoes

Ⓟ Free car park off B6438, ½ mile (800m) west of St Abbs

Ⓣ Minibus service to and from Berwick-upon-Tweed

🍴 Café at Visitor Centre

ᵂᶜ At Visitor Centre

THE WALK

ST ABB'S HEAD – MIRE LOCH

The walk begins at the Nature Reserve car park off the B6438.

➡ Take the path for the Reserve Centre, which leads past a coffee shop, to the end of the garden. Cross the stile and go through a gap in a wall marked by a yellow arrow. Follow a footpath parallel to the road, then turn left down a footpath signposted to St Abb's Head. A gravel path leads to a gate giving access to the cliffs. The path ascends gradually around the back of a bay, with views back to St Abb's Harbour **Ⓐ**, and leads to a viewpoint above White Heugh **Ⓑ**. The path then descends steeply to Burnmouth Harbour and Horsecastle Bay, with the distinct shape of Kirk Hill **Ⓒ** looming ahead. Cross a stile at the back of Horsecastle Bay. Take a path to the left to climb gradually to the gap between Kirk Hill and St Abb's Head.

2 ➡ From here, you can

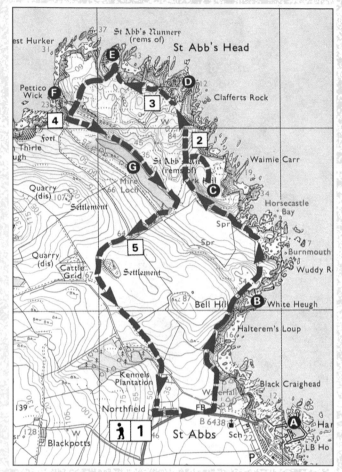

make a detour to your right, along a prominent path to Kirk Hill's summit, and return down the same path. Alternatively, bear

left onto another track and you soon come to St Abb's Head lighthouse **Ⓓ**.

3 ➡ Pass to the left of the lighthouse and drop down

to a metalled road with a small car park. From here, you can explore the spectacular cliffs and inlets north-west of the lighthouse. A gap in the fence allows access to Nunnery Point **Ⓔ**. Continue around the cliff tops, following sheep paths towards Pettico Wick **Ⓕ**. Descend an obvious gully through a line of crags on a very steep grassy slope, or, if you prefer, you can avoid the gully and reach the road higher up by walking over a grassy rise above the crags.

4 ➡ From the bottom of the hill, leave the road and follow a path along the left (north-eastern) side of Mire Loch **Ⓖ**. At the far end, a narrow sheep path drops down to the reeds and leads to the end of the loch, by the dam and water sluice. Cross the sluice and go over a stile. Follow a faint path to a track, then turn right and ascend steeply to the road.

5 ➡ Turn left along the road and follow it back to the car park where the walk began.

kelp at low tide. Further up the shore are common seaweeds, such as bladder wrack.

The black coating on the rocks of the beach is a seawater-resistant lichen. Rock surfaces out of reach of the waves are covered with yellow and green lichens typical of sea cliffs. Also here, are flowering plants such as thrift and sea campion, which can tolerate salt spray.

The sward behind the bay is rich in grasses and wild flowers and is a good area for spotting common blue and meadow brown butterflies. Other butterflies on the reserve include the small copper, the

◀*St Abb's Harbour is still a working port, with crabbers working the coast and other boats trawling further out.*

ALL PHOTOS: JEFFREY BEAZLEY

grayling and migrant species such as the Camberwell beauty. There are also large, day-flying moths and you might see the death's head hawk-moth, a spectacular migrant.

RARE BUTTERFLY

Soon you skirt the south-western slopes of Kirk Hill **C**, sections of which have been fenced off to prevent sheep grazing. This has allowed the growth of rock rose, the main food plant of the caterpillar of the northern brown argus, which is a nationally rare butterfly. After an

▲ *White Heugh, just north of the harbour, is a craggy promontory with various seabirds nesting on its ledges.*

▶ *Kirk Hill from White Heugh. There is a ruined chapel here, and a part of the area is managed for the northern brown argus butterfly. You can climb to the top or skirt round the hill (below).*

optional detour to the top of the hill, the path leads round the cliffs once more to St Abb's Head, the objective of the walk, and the lighthouse **D**, built on the headland in 1862.

When visibility is poor, a large foghorn echoes eerily around the cliffs. The lighthouse is one of the main markers on the approaches to the Firth of Forth. On a clear day here you can see Bass Rock, where there is a huge gannetry, further up the coast towards the Firth of Forth. Gannets can often be seen fishing off St Abb's Head.

The greatest concentration of St Abb's Head's 50,000 or so seabirds is on the cliffs and stacks to the north-west of the lighthouse. The majority are kittiwakes and guillemots, but there are also fulmars, herring gulls, razorbills, shags and a few puffins. Shags are present all year round, but most of the birds leave at the end of July and do not return until the following spring.

LIVING ON THE EDGE

The ancient volcanic rocks of the headland have formed sheer cliffs and pinnacles with many ledges. These are perfect nesting sites, offering access to the sea while being out of the reach of predators, such as foxes. Guillemots and razorbills in particular need a clear drop into the water because the young leave the nest before they have learned to fly. They tumble into the water and swim immediately, but do not take to the air for several more weeks.

All around St Abb's Head, the sea is very rich in plant and animal life, with an unusual mix of Arctic and Atlantic species. This is due to an eddy of the North Atlantic Drift, which swings around north-east Scotland and down the east coast. The clear water and spectacular scenery here make it one the best subaqua locations in Britain.

CONSERVATION

The Voluntary Marine Reserve here was officially opened by Professor David Bellamy in 1984, with the aim of conserving the outstanding biological richness of these inshore waters and to actively encourage

SIMON FRASER

◄ *The squat lighthouse on St Abbs Head functions no matter what the weather. Note the foghorn pointing out to sea.*

responsible educational and recreational use of them alongside the traditional fishing trade.

A little further round the cliffs from the lighthouse is Nunnery Point ❸. The ancient remains here are not as old as was once supposed. Experts now believe that they are not those of a 7th-century nunnery, but those of a more recent, medieval, construction.

PETTICO WICK

After following sheep tracks along the grassy cliff tops, you come to Pettico Wick ❻, where the underlying geology of St Abb's Head is at its most obvious. Stretching westwards is a succession of grey, banded cliffs

▼ *On the west side of St Abb's Head, the small harbour at Pettico Wick is well sheltered from strong easterlies.*

JEFFREY BEAZLEY/AA PHOTO LIBRARY

of rock, laid down some 450 million years ago as mud at the bottom of an ocean. These sediments have been twisted and contorted by immense geological forces, but do not generally provide steep enough cliffs to make them attractive to seabirds. Many of them also have beaches below, and so are not suit-

able for guillemots and razorbills.

The rock is of a fundamentally different type to that found at St Abb's Head, which was formed by volcanic eruptions a mere 50 million years ago. The line between them is an ancient earth movement, the St Abb's Head fault. Pettico Wick lies right on the fault line.

HEADING INLAND

Leaving the sea behind, the route heads inland to the very different habitat around Mire Loch ❼. Formed by a dam built around 1900, the loch lies in a valley that was scoured out by meltwater flowing along the St Abb's Head fault as the glaciers retreated at the end of the last Ice Age. The high crags above the loch contain some rare plants such as spring sandwort and soft clover. Wheatears nest in rabbit burrows on the lower slopes and mute swans, little grebes and kittiwakes can all be found on the loch.

Holy Headland

St Abb's Head takes its name from Aebbe (alternatively known as Ebba or Abb), the daughter of King Edilfred of Northumbria. The story goes that after she was shipwrecked under its cliffs in the 7th century, she believed herself to have been saved by a miracle. By way of thanks, she set up a nunnery and lived the rest of her life as an abbess.

Of the many pilgrims to visit the nunnery, perhaps the most distinguished was St Cuthbert in AD661. He is said to have stood for a whole night in the sea praying, up to his neck in water and surrounded by seals, which swam around him.

The remains at Nunnery Point, north-west of the lighthouse, were once thought to be those of the nunnery, but are now thought to date back only as far as medieval times. It is probable that the nunnery was sited near the ruined medieval chapel on Kirk Hill, where recent archaeological exploration has revealed evidence of a much older settlement on the summit.

NATIONAL TRUST FOR SCOTLAND

Understandably, there are few images of the 7th-century St Abb. This stone carving is at Northfield House, a National Trust for Scotland property near St Abb's Head.

OVER THE BORDER

A strenuous hill walk through the remote and beautiful Cheviots

The walk starts just to the south-east of the settlement of Mowhaugh. After crossing the river by a footbridge, you take a track uphill through several fields. As you gain height, views open out over the valley, which is dotted with farms, and across the rolling hills and their scattered conifer plantations.

SHELTER FROM THE WIND

After less than a mile (1.6km) of gradual ascent, the path enters an L-shaped plantation **A** on the slopes of Swindon Hill. The woods provide shelter from the prevailing winds that blow across these exposed hills. The path continues along the edge of the plantation, frequently crossing fallen trees or branches. The densely-planted conifers can seem oppressive after the open spaces, and the distance sometimes feels further than the map indicates.

Eventually you emerge in open countryside, with an ever expanding panorama of hills on all sides.

▲ *Clennell Street, the old drove road down which mountain cattle were driven to the rich pastures of Norfolk to be fattened for market. A young black darter dragonfly (left) will turn darker when mature. It likes boggy pools.*

The tallest peak, at 2,674 feet (815m), is that of The Cheviot itself, which is a deceptive 5 miles (8km) away to the east. At first it is hard to grasp the scale of these hills, for although they are modest in height, distances are considerable and a quick check on the map will often show landmarks to be much further away than they appear. The landscape evokes a sense of great space and solitude, a great attraction of the area.

SHEEP'S-EYE VIEW

The route climbs Windy Rig, a windswept expanse of tussock-grass, grazed by sheep. There are extensive views here: to the north are the outlying ridges of the Cheviots and the flat lands beyond; to the east is a deep valley; and to the south, the steep slopes of Windy Gyle, the main objective of the walk, are clearly visible.

You follow a fence all the way to the border ridge, passing through a gate into England. The deep valley to the south of the Pennine Way leads to Upper Coquetdale in Northumberland. After crossing over a stile back into Scotland, you follow the Pennine Way to the top of Windy Gyle. The summit **B**, at 2,032

feet (619m), is marked by a large pile of stones, Russell's Cairn, and an Ordnance Survey triangulation point. Simple stone wind-breaks give some shelter from the elements while you take a well-earned rest.

The route continues easily along the border for just over a mile (1.6km), on peaty ground that is frequently wet and boggy, particularly in winter. Clennell Street **C**, an old drovers' road, crosses the border and is clearly marked by a signpost. This is a superb, firm path that leads quickly down through rough pasture to Cocklawfoot.

DROVERS' ROAD

This route was used for centuries for driving cattle reared in Scotland to markets in the south. The trade peaked in the late 18th century, when many thousands of beasts were herded along here every year.

Returning along a metalled road to the start of the walk, you pass several farmsteads, nestled in the shelter of the valley of Cocklawfoot Burn, as well as the sites of several prehistoric settlements.

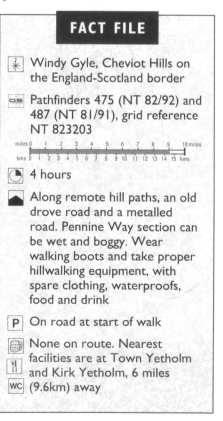

FACT FILE

- ✳ Windy Gyle, Cheviot Hills on the England-Scotland border

- ▱ Pathfinders 475 (NT 82/92) and 487 (NT 81/91), grid reference NT 823203

  miles 0 1 2 3 4 5 6 7 8 9 10 miles
  kms 0 1 2 3 4 5 6 7 8 9 10 11 12 13 14 15 kms

- ◔ 4 hours

- ▲ Along remote hill paths, an old drove road and a metalled road. Pennine Way section can be wet and boggy. Wear walking boots and take proper hillwalking equipment, with spare clothing, waterproofs, food and drink

- Ⓟ On road at start of walk

- 🏠 None on route. Nearest facilities are at Town Yetholm and Kirk Yetholm, 6 miles (9.6km) away
  🍴
  WC

THE WALK

BOWMONT WATER – WINDY GYLE – COCKLAWFOOT

break crossing the path, go diagonally right and into the forest again, through open trees where the path is not so clear as before. As the forest thickens, the path gets more distinct. Eventually, at the end of the forest, you reach a gate through a wire fence.

2 Go through the gate and follow an indistinct path across tussock-grass, keeping a stone wall on your right. After descending a little way, the path becomes a distinct sheep track, which you follow all the way up the gradual ascent of Windy Rig, keeping close to the wall, then a fence. At the border fence, go through a gate to the English side and turn left onto the Pennine Way.

After ascending a little way, cross a stile back to the Scottish side and follow the distinct path to the summit of Windy Gyle **B**.

3 Go down the other side of Windy Gyle and follow the border for about a mile (1.6km) on boggy terrain, going through a gate by a large cairn and continuing to another fence, with a wooden signpost. Cross the stile on your right, then go through the gate on your left, heading north along Clennell Street **C**.

4 After about 2 miles (3.2km) on this good, distinct path, bear right onto the road and follow it for a further 2 miles (3.2km) back to the start.

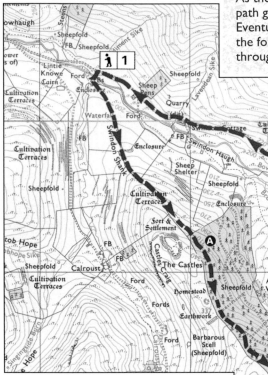

The walk begins about 5 miles (8km) along a minor road heading due south from Primsidemill, which is 1 mile (1.6km) south of Town Yetholm on the B6401. Park near a small wooden hut beside the road, where a footbridge leads across Bowmont Water to a house.

1 Cross the bridge and follow the path a short way to a track. Turn left along this behind the house and uphill to Swindon Shank, a stone enclosure on your left. Bear left to a gate leading to a path along the left-hand (east) side of a stone wall. Continue to the forest plantation **A**, entering it by a forest fire warning sign. The path leads through the plantation, crossing fallen trees that are easily avoided. At a large fire-

BESIDE THE TWEED

JASON SMALLEY. INSET: DUNCAN MCEWAN/AQUILA

On early summer evenings, the river bubbles and boils with trout rising to flies. From September to November, the autumn spate raises the water level sufficiently for salmon to migrate upstream from the open sea; in October especially, the heavy splash of leaping fish echoes along the riverbank.

NEIDPATH CASTLE

On a rocky outcrop above a sweeping bend in the river stands the 13th-century Neidpath Castle **B**, guarding the entrance to Peebles. A stark, forbidding tower, it was besieged by Cromwell in 1650, and damage done by the Parliamentarians' cannons can still be seen in the south-west corner.

Beautifully restored in recent years by the Earl of Wemyss and March, the castle is open to the public in season, and well worth a visit. Its balconies look along the

◄*Through the trees lining the banks of the River Tweed, there is a good view of Neidpath Castle. The effects of conifer forests and acid rain have reduced the survival of salmon parr (inset).*

A stroll along the banks of a romantic salmon river

The Royal Borough of Peebles lies in the Scottish lowlands, sheltered by the wooded hills of Glentress Forest to the north. The knitwear produced here is of world renown, and the town can lay claim to being not only the first, but also the most delightful on the Tweed.

In medieval times, Peebles was famous for its Beltane Festival, a Celtic survival celebrated at the beginning of May. Robert the Bruce, a supporter of all things Celtic, granted the town an annual Beltane

fair. Now held in the last week in June, the Beltane Festival is still a great occasion in the town's calendar, and includes the 'Riding of the Marches', when horsemen beat the common land's boundaries, and the crowning of a Beltane Queen.

The walk begins at Peebles' Tweed Bridge, a splendid five-arched span dating from the late 15th century, and follows the banks of the Tweed **A**, one of Scotland's foremost fishing rivers. The coat of arms of Peebles bears three salmon and the motto 'Against the stream they multiply', a testimony to the quality of Tweed water, which supports 16 species of fish. This stretch of the river is a designated Site of Special Scientific Interest.

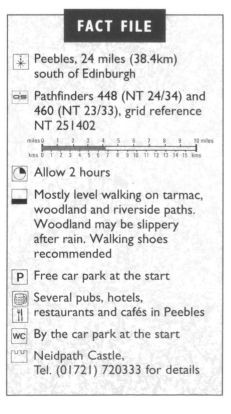

FACT FILE

- ✳ Peebles, 24 miles (38.4km) south of Edinburgh

- 🗺 Pathfinders 448 (NT 24/34) and 460 (NT 23/33), grid reference NT 251402

  miles 0 1 2 3 4 5 6 7 8 9 10 miles
  kms 0 1 2 3 4 5 6 7 8 9 10 11 12 13 14 15 kms

- 🕐 Allow 2 hours

- ▭ Mostly level walking on tarmac, woodland and riverside paths. Woodland may be slippery after rain. Walking shoes recommended

- 🅿 Free car park at the start

- 🍴 Several pubs, hotels, restaurants and cafés in Peebles

- WC By the car park at the start

- 🏰 Neidpath Castle, Tel. (01721) 720333 for details

THE WALK

PEEBLES – MANOR BRIDGE

The walk begins at the riverside car park off the B7062 just south of the Tweed Bridge.

1 Head towards the river and turn left on the riverside path to the Tweed Bridge. Climb the steps to the main road, and turn right across the bridge. At the far side, cross the road and turn left down a tarmac road by the Bridge Inn. Beyond the swimming pool, turn left on the gravel area to the River Tweed **A**.

2 Turn right along the riverside path, soon crossing a footbridge. Climb the steps and turn sharp left at the top, then descend a second set of steps to rejoin the riverside path.

3 Follow the path through Hay Lodge Park over a plank bridge and along a dirt path. Continue past Neidpath Castle **B** on the right. At the railway viaduct **C**, climb the steps and turn right on a broad path (the old railway line) to Manor Bridge.

4 Cross the stile and turn left across the bridge, then go ahead along the tarmac road. Turn left at a junction to cross Old Manor Bridge. Go ahead to the car park viewpoint. Turn left directly opposite onto a woodland path, and proceed downhill, following a dry-stone wall to the lower riverside path.

5 Turn right and follow the path through South Park Wood **D**, past the railway viaduct on your left and the entrance to the tunnel on your right. Continue on the riverside path past Artists' Rock **E** to return to Peebles. At the Tweed Bridge, go up the steps, cross the road to a gate and return to the car park at the starting point of the walk.

course of the Tweed through Peebles, and far into the hills beyond, while its once formal gardens, laid out in wide terraces, slope gently down to the river. The castle also has a resident ghost, a 'white lady' whose identity remains a mystery.

EERIE TUNNEL

Further on, the splendid, seven-arched, Victorian railway viaduct **C** was opened in 1864 to extend the Biggar, Broughton and Symington line into Peebles. Never a commercial success, the passenger service closed in 1950. On the other side of the bridge, the disused line runs beneath South Park Wood through an eerie ½-mile (800-m) tunnel.

At Manor Bridge, the Manor Water enters the Tweed. A century ago, poachers practised the 'sport' of burning the water here; they gathered by torchlight to slaughter the spawning salmon in their hundreds with long-handled tridents. Poaching remains a problem on the Tweed and its tributaries, compounded by the depredations of the mink, an unwelcome alien which scoops salmon onto the moonlit banks.

The path crosses Manor Bridge and follows the gentle contours of the river back through South Park Wood **D**, a richly-mixed plantation of oak, elm, alder, silver birch, larch, spruce and poplar. The wood is an ideal habitat for treecreepers, great spotted woodpeckers, goldcrests and waxwings. Red squirrels chew noisily on fir cones, secure in their compact dreys 20 feet (6m) above the forest floor in the forks between tree trunk and side-branches.

ARTISTS' ROCK

On the opposite bank of the river to Neidpath is Artists' Rock **E**, where generations have sat and sketched the castle. The reprobate 4th Duke of Queensberry destroyed Neidpath's terraces as an act of malice towards his heir, and felled the surrounding trees to finance his extravagant London lifestyle. Fortunately he failed to completely destroy this fine view. A short stroll along the bank takes you back to the start.

◀*As you return towards Peebles along the lush, verdant riverbank, the scene is one of timeless tranquillity.*

JASON SMALLEY

BRAVE BORDERLAND

Around a loch steeped in the tumultuous history of the Borders

▲ *Fierce-looking but harmless Highland cattle graze the grasslands at the loch's edge near Bowerhope Farm. The mountain hare (inset), which has a white coat in winter, occurs by the loch.*

In the heart of the Borderland's great Ettrick Forest lies the 'valley of the silent loch', an inspiration to Wordsworth, Burns, Scott and Hogg and a refuge to the hunted men of the Covenant. Here, the hills hold memories of brave Borderers, who still haunt the rugged glens and cleuchs (cloughs) beyond the lonely shores of St Mary's Loch.

The route begins on the banks of the Loch of Lowes, where gentle blue waves lap the pebbled beach. Nearby is James Hogg's monument Ⓐ. The poet's benign face gazes out across the loch he lovingly immortalized in verse, while his sheepdog keeps a watchful eye on the black-faced ewes that crop the sward beneath his master's feet.

The route continues along the banks of St Mary's Loch Ⓑ. Many Scottish lochs are tinged with peaty deposits, but these waters are exceptionally clear. This is a Site of Special Scientific Interest, one of the largest natural water reserves in southern Scotland. It was carved from the mountainous terrain by the glaciers that marched down Yarrow Water, gouging out the valley bottom to the loch's present depth of 150 feet (45m). Popular throughout the summer with hikers, fishermen and sailing enthusiasts, in winter the valley and the loch can be desolate.

Cappercleuch's church Ⓒ nestles on the hillside above Megget Water. Remote and tiny, it owes its name to the capercaillie, the 'old man of the wood', though many years have passed since this huge grouse inhabited the surrounding hills.

Just over ¾ mile (1.2km) further

FACT FILE

✳ St Mary's Loch, 18 miles (28.8km) west of Selkirk, on the A708

▭ Pathfinder 472 (NT 22/32), grid reference NT 238204

miles 0 1 2 3 4 5 6 7 8 9 10 miles
kms 0 1 2 3 4 5 6 7 8 9 10 11 12 13 14 15 kms

◔ Allow 4 hours

▭ Mostly easy walking on level footpaths, tarmac and forestry roads. One steep climb, to the churchyard. Some shallow streams to cross, and a few muddy sections. Walking boots are recommended

P At the start

▭ Tibbie Shiels Inn and The Rodono Hotel

⑂ Snacks at the Glen Café (holiday season only)

WC Next to the Glen Café

JASON SMALLEY. INSET: L CAMPBELL/NHPA

THE WALK

ST MARY'S LOCH

The walk starts from a parking field on the north shore of the Loch of the Lowes, opposite the Glen Café.

1 Leave the car park and turn right along the main road (A708). Shortly, turn left to cross a field up to the Hogg memorial **Ⓐ**. Retrace your steps to the main road. Turn left and follow it for about ½ mile (800m) along the shore of St Mary's Loch **Ⓑ** to pass a white cottage on your right and a stone one almost opposite on your left.

2 About 50 yards (45m) further on, bear left, uphill to a gate into the forestry. Follow the forest path through to the Rodono Hotel. Go straight on through the Hotel car park to a wooden fence with a step stile onto a footbridge. Bear left after the footbridge up a short incline, then right onto a path roughly parallel with the road and loch. At a fork, bear right down towards the road and follow the line of the

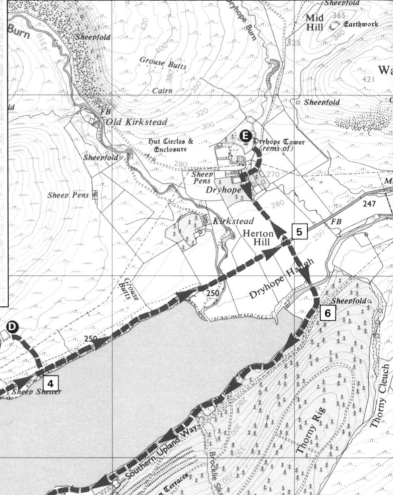

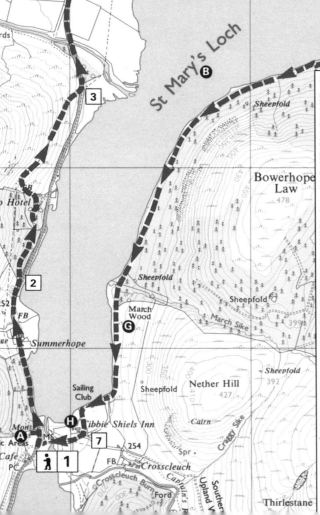

fence to a gate.

3 Go through the gate and turn left along the road over Megget Water bridge and through Cappercleuch, passing the church **Ⓒ** on your left and the village hall on your right.

4 After approximately 1½ miles (2.4km) turn left at a signpost for St Marie's Kirkyard. Cross the step stile and go straight on up the hill to the churchyard **Ⓓ**. Retrace your steps to a crossroads of broad paths just before the step stile. Turn left and follow a broad path through a field gate, across a shallow burn and through a second and a third gate. Keep ahead on

the broad path until you come to a stone wall. Bear right down to a gate, go through it and turn left along the road.

5 At a crossroads by a small lodge, turn left up the farm track. Keep straight on past the farm buildings. Bear right past a gate, then left after a second gate to cross a field to Dryhope Tower **Ⓔ**. Retrace your steps to the crossroads and go straight on over the road. Cross a cattle grid onto a tarmac drive and continue straight ahead through a gate and over a bridge onto a forestry road.

6 Follow the forestry road, ignoring a fork to the

ALL PHOTOS: JASON SMALLEY

◄*Cappercleuch's neat church nestles below the boggy moorland of Capper Law. The water that runs off the surrounding hills ensures that St Mary's Loch (right) and two further reservoirs to the west are always full.*

on, the path to St Marie's Kirkyard ❶ leads upwards through bracken, bell heather and pungent cushions of sweet old thyme. St Marie's of the Lowes is a wild, windswept grave-yard whose crumbling tombstones name six centuries of Scotts, Kerrs and Pringles, now slumbering peacefully together — both they and their bitter feuds long forgotten.

A Blanket Preaching Service is held here every July. The origins of the service are obscure; some believe it commemorates the plight of the Covenanters who fulfilled their need to worship as Presbyterians at secret, open air conventicles. They sought sanctuary in these rugged hills and glens, only to be hunted down and slain by the Redcoats.

A small mound just to the east of the Forest Kirk marks the unhal-lowed burial ground of Binram. A

former priest and willing emissary to Claverhouse, he was slain in the kirkyard for his betrayal of the hunted men of the Covenant. His murderers later justified the deed by perpetuating tales of Binram's collu-sion with the devil, earning him the title 'wizard priest'.

PEEL TOWER

Back along the shore, the peace is disturbed by the clamorous cries of a resident colony of black-headed gulls. Even though many of their eggs are removed during the breed-ing season for the benefit of local fishermen, they still manage to maintain a very healthy population.

A path leads from the road up past a farm to Dryhope Tower ❺, an impressive border peel tower. Its walls, 4 feet (1.2m) thick, and strate-gically-placed firing holes made it a virtually impenetrable fortress. This was home of the most infamous Border reiver, Wat Scott of Harden, and his beautiful wife Mary, 'The Flower of Yarrow'. When the larder was empty, Mary would simply serve her husband a dish of spurs — a subtle enough message to send him charging over the border to round up livestock. One night in

▼*Long deserted, the sturdily built Dryhope Tower, once the home of Wat Scott, has survived for over 400 years.*

1596, following a raid in Cumberland, Wat rode home with 300 cattle, 20 horses and the spoils from two looted houses.

The walk crosses a bridge over the River Yarrow. Sluices regulate the flow of water out of the loch so that a constant water level can be maintained. As the path follows the contours of the loch, the gentle hues of larch and wild cherry on your left fringe a 20-year-old plantation of Sitka spruce.

In winter, the rocky escarpment overhead is hung with dagger-sharp

◄*Perched high above the northern shore of the loch, the abandoned St Marie's Kirkyard commands a fine view.*

left, straight on to the gated entrance to a lochside field. Cross the step stile into the field. Leave the farm track to Bowerhope Farmhouse ❻; instead, follow a footpath along the lochside.

Continue on the obvious path, following waymarks away from the lochside for a while, then back to it. Eventually, you come to March Wood ❼. Cross a step stile in the woods. Go over a footbridge and

follow the path as it bears right to a step stile into the sailing club field. Follow the main track in front of the club, round to the left to the gated entrance to Tibbie Shiels Inn ❽. Go through the kissing-gate

and straight on through the car park to a T-junction at the entrance.

➡ Turn right onto the tarmac road and continue over the bridge. Bear left at the fork to return to the car park at the start.

The Ettrick Shepherd

This statue of James Hogg, with his sheepdog at his feet, overlooks St Mary's Loch which he knew so well.

James Hogg, born in Ettrick on 9 December 1770, was an almost uneducated cowherd and shepherd, but his empathy with the traditional ballads and legends of the Borderland led him to become one of Scotland's literary giants. He had only six months' schooling in his life, but as he wandered the wild open moors, his imagination was fired by the tremendous wealth of history and folklore that still bewitches visitors today.

His prodigious talent for poetry led to his introduction to Edinburgh society, where he was initially thought a rustic oddity, but was later appreciated for the simple beauty of his verse. Success allowed him to settle on his own farm. Though he was not as gifted at husbandry as at poetry, Jamie found ample solace in good company, fine music, literature and conversation.

He never aspired to the production of the sophisticated classics of contemporaries such as Sir Walter Scott; his prose and poetry are as honest and raw as the landscape that inspired them.

▲*A farm track drops from Dryhope to the southern shore of the loch.*

icicles, which break and shatter with the thaw, the tinkling music they make echoing across the still water. Snow lies a long time on the north-facing shore, crazily patterned by the feet of mountain hare, fox, weasel, rabbit and vole.

In spring, the banks are dotted with countless pale primroses and rich, velvet-faced dog violets. Roe deer are frequent visitors to the lochside; you can expect to see does and their young cross the path as they bound up from the shoreline into the dense forestry land.

At the end of the road stands Bowerhope Farmhouse ❻. In 1455, Bowerhope was a 'six-pound forest steading in the ward of Ettrick', and the entire area from Carlisle to Edinburgh was part of the great Ettrick Forest, favoured royal hunting ground of the Stuart monarchs.

BURIED ALIVE

In the early 19th century, Alexander Laidlaw was the tenant at Bower-hope. He is remembered for surviving being buried alive in a snowdrift for over 14 hours, and owed his life to his faithful dogs. Two of his descendants were less fortunate. They drowned in St Mary's Loch, one in a rowing boat, the other losing his way in the dark with his horse and trap. Maurice Henry Hewlett, a popular, turn-of-the-century novelist, wrote his romantic tale *The Forest Lovers* at Bowerhope.

From here, there is a highly evocative view of the forsaken Forest Kirkyard of St Marie's, nestling on a plateau between two gushing burns. As one tenant of Bowerhope paused from his hay-making to look across, he thought he saw the dead rising from their graves, their white wraith-like forms swaying in the summer breeze. A night of terrified prayer followed, but dawn revealed the truth. A travelling pedlar, who had fallen in the loch, had hung his soaking lengths of linen and muslin on the tombstones to dry.

The route along the hillside above the loch follows the footsteps of Bonnie Prince Charlie as he marched south to join the ill-fated Highland Army. Short-eared owls, oystercatchers, kestrels and skylarks are a common sight here, and the rough heathland hosts a surprising diversity of wild flowers.

The March Wood ❼ is always a welcome sight, a tiny oasis of Scots Pine on the edge of the loch; the burn running through it is as clear and refreshing as the wildest of mountain tarns. This must surely be where James Hogg wrote his magical poem *Kilmeny* — an ideal place for a tale of fairy enchantment.

COLOURFUL CHARACTER

Beyond the sailing club is a gravelly strip of land that divides St Mary's Loch from the smaller Loch of the Lowes. Here, a short walk from the beginning of the route, stands the Tibbie Shiels Inn ❽, a pub named after its first landlady. A woman of considerable character, she added much to local legend when she came to live here in 1823. Of James Hogg (see box), a regular customer, she said in epitaph; 'He was a gey sensible man for a' the nonsense he wrat'.

◄*When you pass the dinghies of the sailing club, you are close to the Tibbie Shiels Inn at the end of the walk.*

ALL PHOTOS: JASON SMALLEY

THE MISTY ISLE

GEORGE YOUNG PICTURE LIBRARY. INSET: PAUL STERRY/NATURE PHOTOGRAPHERS

▲ *The spectacular isle seen from Seamill on the mainland. (inset) An eider duck is well camouflaged on the beach.*

A moorland and coastal walk on the Isle of Arran

The Isle of Arran, nearly 170 square miles (440 square km) in size, lies in the broad estuary of the Firth of Clyde. The northern tip has majestic mountains where herds of red deer roam and several pairs of

GEORGE YOUNG PICTURE LIBRARY

The raised beach was formed millions of years ago after the Ice Age had ended.

FACT FILE

⚹ North Arran, Isle of Arran

🚉 Pathfinder 441 (NR 94/NS 04), grid reference NR 940504

miles 0   1   2   3   4   5   6   7   8   9   10 miles
kms 0   1   2   3   4   5   6   7   8   9 10 11 12 13 14 15 kms

◕ Allow 4 hours

▲ Not recommended for children or the elderly. Could be difficult in wet weather. Rock scrambling, so walking boots and waterproof clothing essential

P Take side road opposite Loch Ranza Field Centre, close to milestone 44. Cross bridge over Chalmadale Burn and turn left at end of road. Park on verges just beyond Lodge Farm

T Ferry from Ardrossan - Brodick, then bus to Lochranza. Infrequent off-season. Advisable to take early ferry

🍴 Refreshments at camp site before milestone 44 or at any café by jetty. (Not open off-season)

WC Beyond Lochranza jetty

golden eagles hunt their territories. After climbing over moorland slopes and visiting ruined crofts, this walk continues along the shore of one of Arran's raised beaches, passing over a variety of rocks laid down millions of years ago. This walk offers wonderful opportunities to observe the red deer, seals and basking sharks; to look for eagles, ravens, buzzards, cuckoos and peregrines; to watch eider ducks, oyster-catchers and sandpipers; to walk over moorland slopes where cotton grass, sphagnum moss and bog asphodel grow; and to pass wet meadows of butterwort, grass of Parnassus and spotted orchids.

MOORLAND AND SHORE

There is a steady climb at the start of the walk to a boggy, moorland pass Ⓐ 800 feet (240 metres) high, between Tor Meadhonach and Creag Ghlas. To the right lies a disused slate quarry and slates lie scattered over the path. These are Lochranza slates which used to be taken down to the

THE WALK

AROUND THE TIP OF NORTH ARRAN

The walk begins from the parking area by the shore.

1 Walk back along the narrow road from the parking area. Where it bears right continue ahead up a gently sloping track, signposted Cock Farm 4 miles (6.4 km), Laggan 5 miles (8 km). Step out along the track and after ¹/₂ mile (800 metres) turn left on to a grassy path signposted to The Cock and Laggan. This soon becomes a path, bordered with bracken — the haunt of many butterflies, and various dragonflies and grasshoppers.

2 Cross by a narrow, wooden footbridge (take care because the bridge is rotting in places), over the Eadaraidh burn, which is shaded by willow and birch. Stride the steadily climbing path. Away to the right lies the Sleeping Warrior, the mile-long (1.6 km) mountain tops forming the silhouette of a soldier wearing a helmet, lying with his arms folded across his chest. Look for red deer on the slopes about the path.

3 The path continues over a moorland pass **A**. It can be very wet here, but it is possible to pick a way carefully and still remain dryshod.

4 Once the ridge is attained a glorious view (when the weather is good) lies below, of the white topped waves of the Sound of Bute and the mainland misty in the distance. Look across to the nearest island, Inchmarnock, where miscreants were exiled.

5 Follow the lovely path, with care, downhill. Then take a grassy path, steeply sloping downwards, to the left. Follow this through bracken, turning right at its end, and continue to a ruined stone house **B**.

6 Leave the ruined croft and return a few yards along the same path. Continue ahead, passing the path just walked on the left. Follow the wide grassy path as it curves gently down the contours and then levels out to reach Cock Farm **C**.

7 Leave Cock Farm and walk south-east, keeping beside the drystone wall.

village in carts. Below the peaty soil lies impermeable Dalradian schist with bands of slate running through it. This schist is the oldest rock on the island and is said to have been laid down 700 million years ago.

THE BLACK HOUSE

A steeply sloping path leads to a ruined stone house **B**, or croft, with a drystone wall. It would have been thatched with heather and bracken. The windows were very small and they would have had shutters to keep out the rain and snow. Next to the house are the ruins of the cow byre which would have had a connecting door to allow the farmer to reach the animals for milking without going out into the cold. The family would have had to suffer the smell of the animals but would have benefited from their heat.

Cock Farm **C**, also a ruin, was the home of a wealthier family than

The ruins of the castle are a far cry from those of the humble crofts.

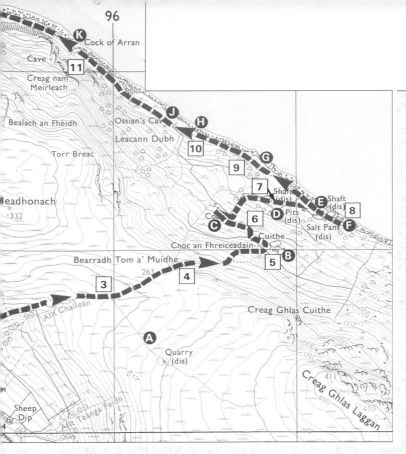

past the flooded mine shaft **E** and the ruined croft where the salt was processed until reaching the tiny Laggan harbour **F** — a few steps beyond.

9 Return past the mine shaft and stride out along the shore path, again wet in places. Look for the red limestone, recognised by its faulting and grooves, and for the fossils of bivalves **G** .

10 Continue on past the red sandstone rocks with layers of angular fragments embedded **H** . A short scramble through a rocky area ensues, then look for the entrance to Ossian's Cave **J** beneath a tall ash tree at the foot of the towering cliffs. It can be reached by a small, muddy path leading off to the left.

11 Continue along this glorious way, where dry, and thread carefully along

the marshy path past the Cock of Arran **K** .

12 Follow the path, with care, as it climbs steadily into An Scriodan **L** . If the tide is out you can avoid the rock fall by walking along the pebbly beach.

13 Step out along the grassy area just above the pebbly shore passing the cottage at Fairy Dell.

14 Continue ahead following the grassy path as it quickly swings left below the cliff **M** . In about ½ mile (800 metres), at the first small stream, walk a few paces right across the bog myrtle and reeds to the shore to see Hutton's Unconformity **N** on the west side of the Allt Beithe.

15 Return to the path and continue ahead, sometimes over marshy ground, until reaching the metalled road at South Newton. The parking area lies ¹/₂ mile (800 metres) ahead.

Follow the path as it drops downhill, steeply at first. Pass through a small wood, stepping across a narrow stream to a marshy area beyond, then over a stone dyke. Continue south-east, then east along the path bordered by bracken, then over a raised beach **D**, through irises and reeds, stepping carefully over the wetter areas until drier ground is reached.

8 At the shore walk on

Pick a fine day to visit Arran or you will miss the views across the loch.

mine shaft used to obtain coal from a thin seam. The coal was used to heat huge cauldrons of salt water and the salt, obtained by evaporation, was used for curing fish.

FOSSIL HUNTING

Laggan harbour **F** was just big enough for the small boats of the busy community living here in the 18th century. On a rock, tilting away from the sea, lies the fossilised track of a giant centipede which is about 3 feet (1 metre) in length. Under this huge sheet of sandstone are layers of black shale with a glistening thin seam of coal embedded between them. It is also worth looking out for fossils of bivalves and coral **G** embedded in red limestone which was laid down in warm shallow seas, possibly as far back as 400 million years ago.

those who lived in the so-called black house. It was the ancestral home of the Macmillan family, which includes Harold Macmillan, Prime Minister from 1957 to 1963, and Daniel, the publisher, who was born here in 1813.

The path along the shore passes over the 265 foot (81 metre) high

raised beach **D**. The sea level was much higher years ago because of the immense weight of ice pressing down on the land. As the ice melted, returning water to the sea, the land rose leaving raised beaches backed by stranded sea cliffs. A deep pool **E** with reinforced walls can be seen beside the path. This was once a

The gloriously smooth red sandstone here is layered with large

Crofting

Crofting was a way of life for many in the Highlands and Islands and the cluster of ruins close to the shore of the north of Arran were once home to some half a dozen families. The traditional crofts were called black houses, because a fire was always kept burning in the middle of the floor and filled the room with peaty smoke. The land was farmed very inefficiently, by the run-rig system. Each year the family would chose, by lot, a number of strips of land but these were often separated by many other strips belonging to neighbouring families.

This type of life was abandoned during the Highland Clearances in the 18th and 19th centuries. There were several reasons for the Clearances. Often there were too many people trying to make a very meagre living from too little land and crop failures made a difficult life even worse.

In addition, many of the landowners evicted the crofters from their homes

One man and his dog outside a traditional croft thatched with heather and bracken.

in order to make more money from sheep farming and, later, deerstalking. The crofters were literally thrown out of their homes and had no choice but to emigrate to places like Canada and the United States, or move to large towns and cities in order to support their families. The Clearances destroyed much of the traditional way of life in the Scottish Highlands. But now some people are beginning to return to crofting.

angular fragments **H** brought down, it is said, 270 million years ago in flash floods. Here too, raised dykes

The mouth of the mysterious Ossian's cave, with strange carvings and paintings.

run across the shore. These are igneous rocks which, when hot, were pushed up from below, then cooled. Once these dykes lay below the surface but now erosion has exposed them.

Ossian's Cave **J**, found at the base of one of the stranded sea cliffs, has faint carvings of ships and dates on its walls, said to be the work of sheltering quarrymen.

The Cock of Arran **K**, a huge boulder of sandstone, once looked like a cockerel crowing. It was used as a landmark by fishermen to guide them ashore; alas, with age, it has now lost its vital head.

FOUNDING FATHER

Further along the route there is a rockfall known as An Scriodan **L**. This was caused when the cliffs collapsed 250 years ago. Huge boulders of sandstone, with stones embedded in them, remain piled high. Beyond a cottage at Fairy Dell the Dalradian schist **M** occurs once again. Here, the aromatic bog myrtle grows in great profusion.

Hutton's Unconformity **N** lies beside the path on the shore. James

Hutton is considered the father of geology. When on a field trip to Arran in 1789 he noticed the unusual formation of rocks meeting at an angle and gave his name to them. They are formed from red sandstone, laid down 400 million years ago, which tilts towards the sea, overlying greenish schist, thought to be about 600 million years old, and dipping inland — a dramatic feature on a very dramatic coastline.

The jagged peaks and rock formations on the Isle of Arran are a real delight for any enthusiastic geologist.

SECRET ISLAND

ROGER SMITH, INSET: LAURIE CAMPBELL/NHPA

▲ *Sunset Sound: Kerrera is perhaps at its most beautiful at this time of day. An otter (inset) forages in the seaweed.*

An interesting and varied walk on an historic island

The West Highland town of Oban is a busy, bustling place, even out of season. As the main ferry terminal to the Isle of Mull and many of the Inner Hebridean islands, it is more than just a popular tourist haunt. Although its popularity is well justified for its position around Oban Bay, the views, looking out towards the distant Isle of Mull, arc scenically splendid and have become internationally renowned.

Contributing to that scenic splendour, and protecting the town from the vagaries of the open sea, the Isle of Kerrera stretches its green and rugged back across the mouth of the bay. It looks an attractive island, with its hummocky hills and rocky bays, and portrays an atmosphere of Hebridean tranquillity.

Probably because of its close proximity to the tourist trap of Oban, few visitors bother to make the short crossing to savour the peace and quiet, and the history, of this beautiful island.

A small ferry crosses the Sound of Kerrera at frequent intervals every day. Just 2 miles (3.2 km) south of Oban on the Gallanach road you will come across the 'Kerrera Ferry' signpost, and a large, square sign which you have to turn round to

---

FACT FILE

⚹ Kerrera, Strathclyde, Scotland

⊟ Pathfinders 344 and 343 (NM 82/92 and NM 62/72), grid reference NM 830286

miles 0   1   2   3   4   5   6   7   8   9   10 miles
kms 0   1   2   3   4   5   6   7   8   9   10   11   12   13   14   15 kms

🕐 Allow 3 hours

▭ Fairly easy walking on footpaths, minor roads, grass and shoreline. Waterproof boots are recommended

T The Island of Kerrera is reached by ferry from Gallanach, 2 miles (3.2km) south of Oban

P There is a car parking space beside the ferry point

🍴 There are no facilities on the island. Oban, however, is well
WC served by hotels, restaurants, cafés and public toilets

THE WALK

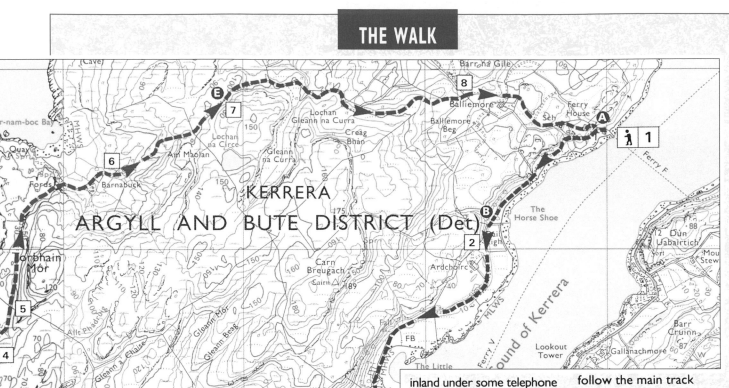

THE ISLE OF KERRERA

The walk begins at Port Kerrera Ferry slip **A**.

1 Turn left below the ferry house by the telephone box and then turn left again at a junction of some farm tracks. Follow the unsurfaced road in a southerly direction towards Horseshoe Bay and Dail Righ **B**.

2 Continue past Little Horseshoe, and Upper Gylen to Lower Gylen. Go through a gate on the left just before Upper Gylen farmhouse and follow the track to Gylen Castle **C**.

3 Return to the Lower Gylen and continue to Orasaig **D**, keeping right,

inland under some telephone wires, then bear right again at a fork. At a wire fence, take the path on the left that is signposted to a ferry, crossing the burn (stream) by a simple wooden bridge. Turn north towards the old house at Ardmore, bearing left between wooden posts, following the line of the glen and ignoring some tracks which go off to the left.

4 At the summit of a pass take the track to the right of a small, overgrown loch. Cross a burn, pass a pile of boulders, then cross another burn by stepping stones.

5 Pass through a gate in a wire fence and carry straight on. Where the track forks, keep right and

follow the main track around the foot of the hill.

6 Bear inland now towards the white farmhouse of Barnabuck, then take the line of the old stone wall in front of it.

7 Reach some old houses and take the grassy road **E** up the hill to the right. Follow the track round some tight bends then straight on for about 1/2 mile (800 metres).

8 Go through a gate and straight on, ignoring the farm road on the left. In 200 yards (180 metres) go through a second gate, continue straight on, through another gate, and pass the school on the right. Follow the road back to the ferry.

◄ *The old drove road near Barnabuck is now empty of the huge herds of cattle that came this way to market.*

ROGER SMITH

indicate to the ferryman on Kerrera that there is a visitor waiting to cross. In these days of computerized communication it is a quaint method of hailing your transport and it is a system that works remarkably well. The yellow oilskin-clad ferryman makes the crossing

several times a day, even in bad conditions. But pick your crossing time carefully because the boatman goes off for his lunch every day.

It is a short crossing, and in a few minutes you will be landing at the grandly named Port Kerrera **A**: a couple of houses, a church and a lone, red telephone box.

Climb the hill and turn left just below the Ferry House to take a tour of the southern, and the most

▲ *The sandpiper calls a loud 'twi-wi-wi-wee when it takes off. Kerrera Sound (left) — shelter for longships.*

interesting part of the island.

Soon you will reach the wide Horseshoe Bay and the Dail Righ **B**, or the King's Field, where Alexander II of Scotland died during a royal visit in 1249. He was endeavouring to assert his rights as king in this district, at a time when this part of Scotland regarded Norway as its mother country.

As you wander southwards, enjoy the view over the Sound of Kerrera. In 1263 King Hakon of Norway arrived here with over 160 longships. The Vikings controlled most of the Hebridean waters, and this powerful host sheltered here before sailing on to be defeated at the Battle of Largs. That defeat was the beginning of the end of Viking sovereignty in the Hebrides, although even today their influence is still recognised in place names.

THE BROOCH OF LORN

Further south, a subsidiary track leaves the main one and trickles down to the impressive ruins of Gylen Castle **C**. Perched high on its cliffs overlooking Castle Bay and the open sea, it dominates the surroundings. This ancient tower, built in 1352 by the MacDougalls of

Dunollie, was ransacked by troops under the command of one Campbell of Bragleen in 1647. Among the booty stolen was the famous 'Brooch of Lorn' — a priceless piece of jewellery that had been taken centuries ealier in 1306 by the MacDougalls from Robert the Bruce during the Battle of Dalrigh, near Tyndrum,

and stored in the castle.

The Bruce wore the brooch on his cloak and, so legend goes, one of MacDougall's followers managed to lay hands on the king, but died of a hefty blow dealt from the royal claymore for his rashness. With his dying grasp though, the clansman managed to tear the king's cloak from his shoulders and with it, the shoulder brooch.

The brooch was later found and taken to Gylen Castle for safekeeping and there it remained for over 300 years.

After it was taken from the castle it remained the spoil of Campbell of Inverawe and in 1826 was gener-

▼ *Port a' Chasteil near Gylen Castle is an impressive but secluded rocky inlet.*

▲ *The ruins of Gylen Castle, home of the Brooch of Lorn for 300 years, still dominate their dramatic surroundings.*

ROGER SMITH

ously presented to the MacDougall family who have owned it ever since. The large crystal which is set in the brooch is said to be extremely unusual. It seems that a warm glow emanates from the stone under any lighting conditions. Surrounding the crystal are a number of pearls set in a circle. Another very unusual feature of the brooch is a small box that is revealed when the centre of the brooch is unscrewed. Inside the box is a tiny piece of bone, which is thought to be a relic of some distant saint and also a small, faded piece of the MacDougall tartan.

The remains of Gylen Castle are set in truly dramatic surroundings. Backed by a landscape of rocky outcrops it offers magnificent seaward views that extend from the mountains of Mull, on the right, to the smaller islands in the Firth of Lorne,

such as Seil, Scarba and the Garvellachs, much loved by Saint Columba. Legend claims that the saint brought his mother here from Ulster, where she set up a nunnery on one of the small islands.

CATTLE DROVERS

At the most southerly part of the walk at Port Dubh of Orasaig **D**, an ancient drove road takes you back over the rugged spine of the island to Balliemore and Port Kerrera and the ferry. At one time huge herds of cattle were landed here from Mull on their way to the huge trysts at Crieff and Falkirk in the south. The route taken by the cattle herdsmen and their beasts is now a fine 'green road' **E** offering wonderful views across to Lismore, Mull and the Garvellachs, the 'Isles of the Sea', and the hills of Morvern.

The Norse Influence

In the summer of 794, Viking longships were first seen in Scottish waters. All the coasts of Scotland and much of the north of England were ravaged by the warlike Norsemen, and for the next 80-100 years the attacks continued with seasonal regularity.

An economic crisis in Norway, cause by a sudden population explosion, led many Norsemen to take to the sea to make a living from piracy, slave trading and raiding foreign shores. The Hebrides, the northern Isles, the Irish Isles and the Isle of Man made fair targets.

Later, in 872, Harold Haarfager became king and he imposed a feudal system on his country which many landowners rebelled against. They, in turn, left Norway and settled in the Hebrides, Orkney and Shetland and the Caithness coast from where they regularly attacked the coast of Norway.

Harold, in turn, brought together a great fleet of longships and took the islands, leaving behind *jarls* (or viceroys) as local rulers. At the height of their power they ruled all the Hebrides, almost all of Argyll and the north of Scotland as far south as Inverness.

Around 1130, Somerled (whose mother was Norse), then the Lord of the Isles, drove the Vikings out of mainland Argyll (which is now Highland

MARY EVANS PICTURE LIBRARY

Region). In 1156 he defeated a Norse battle fleet near Islay. Eventually, King Hakon of Norway was goaded into an expedition to Scotland and in 1263 he sailed with 120 ships as far south as Largs on the Firth of Clyde. During the battle, fought in a westerly gale, his men were routed and many of his ships

Long before Britannia ruled the waves, the fierce and warlike Norsemen dominated both land and sea in the Highlands and Islands for hundreds of years until they were ousted by Somerled.

were wrecked. This defeat led to Norway finally giving up the Hebrides after over 400 years.

THE CRINAN CANAL

FORESTRY COMMISSION, EDINBURGH. INSET: ANDREW CLEAVE/NATURE PHOTOGRAPHERS LTD

A fine forest walk, leading to the superb viewpoint of Knapdale

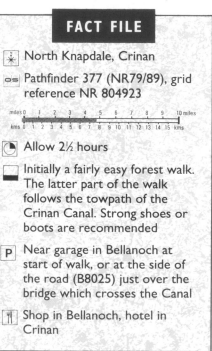

▲Dunardry viewpoint offers superb vistas across the Crinan Canal to the River Add and Loch Crinan. Moorland streams in these environments are the perfect habitat for golden rod (left).

This walk offers a good introduction to the Knapdale area and follows Forestry Commission tracks on the northern fringe of the Knapdale forest. From many points on the walk there are extensive views to distant Cruachan Beinn in the north and the Paps of Jura in the south west, while closer at hand lies the flat and fertile plain of the Moine Mhor, the Great Moss where the ancient rock of Dunadd stands.

The ruin of a fort on the summit of this rock is one of many ancient artifacts to be found in the area; indeed history recalls that many of the early kings of Scotland were crowned here in the ancient fort. The walk finishes with a traverse of the Crinan Canal towpath from Cairnbann to Bellanoch.

In the south west corner of the old county of Argyll, just north of the long peninsula of the Mull of Kintyre, the lands of Knapdale stretch south-westwards like great knuckles and fingers. Sea lochs bite deep into the land, penetrating this area of low knobbly hills and long wooded valleys. The area is said to derive its name from the Norse 'knappr dair' which apparently describes the topography of the area — a low rocky peninsula.

THE SOUND OF JURA

In the north of the district the land mass is broken up into long, low promontories by the sea lochs, while South Knapdale is made up of an expansive lochan-studded plateau, bounded in the east by Loch Fyne, in the west by the Sound of Jura and in the south by West Loch Tarbert. Only a narrow neck of land between Loch Fyne and West Loch Tarbert

FACT FILE

☀ North Knapdale, Crinan

⊟ Pathfinder 377 (NR79/89), grid reference NR 804923

miles 0 1 2 3 4 5 6 7 8 9 10 miles
kms 0 1 2 3 4 5 6 7 8 9 10 11 12 13 14 15 kms

◗ Allow 2½ hours

▭ Initially a fairly easy forest walk. The latter part of the walk follows the towpath of the Crinan Canal. Strong shoes or boots are recommended

P Near garage in Bellanoch at start of walk, or at the side of the road (B8025) just over the bridge which crosses the Canal

⊪ Shop in Bellanoch, hotel in Crinan

THE WALK

BALLANOCK – KNAPDALE – CRINAN CANAL

The walk begins at the tiny village of Bellanoch, on the B841 Lochgilphead to Crinan Road.

1▶ With the Crinan Canal on your left follow the B841 towards Lochgilphead for just over ¼ mile (400 metres).

2▶ Just after where the road bends slightly to the left, leave it and follow the obvious forestry track on the right that winds its way uphill quite steeply.

3▶ After 200 yards (180 metres) on the track a junction is reached. Turn left through the gate. Continue on the track for about 300 yards (275 metres).

4▶ Another junction is reached. Turn left this time and continue for about 600 yards (550 metres).

5▶ At the next junction, a T-junction, turn right and follow a rough path that appears to be extremely over-grown. A line of power cables runs alongside this path. Continue on the path until you reach the house called Dunans.

6▶ Continue on a wide forest track with fine views behind you over the Knapdale Forest. Ignore turns to the right and then to the left – stay on the main track.

7▶ Soon the path begins to bend right in front of a small quarry. Just before the quarry, climb up a waymarked path to reach the view point of Dunardry **A**. Look south-west for a fine view across the Paps of Jura, and north for the view across the Moine Mhor **B** and to the rock of Dunadd **C**. Return to the main path.

8▶ Keep left at the next junction and after 150 yards (135 metres) a yellow waymarker points out a narrow footpath through the forest. Follow this path, which soon drops to another forest track.

9▶ Turn right at the main track and follow this to a car park.

10▶ Turn left onto the main road. A short distance to the right is the village of Cairnbaan **D**. The route continues to the left, though, along the road. After the first house cross the canal lock to reach the towpath of the Crinan Canal **E**.

11▶ Continue past the Dunardry Rolling Bridge **F** and follow the towpath back to Bellanoch.

offers a tenuous link to the long Mull of Kintyre.

Technically the areas of Knapdale and the Mull of Kintyre together form an island, for the finger of land that connects Knapdale to mid-Argyll is sliced by the man-made waterway of the Crinan Canal. Designed by John Rennie and opened in 1801, it runs for some 9 miles (14 km) between Ardrishaig and Crinan and the canal towpath offers a delightful walking route with views across the flat Moine

▶ *The Crinan Canal changes in character along its length. Below Dunardry, it is wooded and peaceful. At its north end, in the Crinan Basin (below), it provides mooring for yachts and fishing boats.*

FORESTRY COMMISSION, EDINBURGH

STB/STILL MOVING PICTURE LIBRARY

Mhor to the great rock of Dunadd and southwards to the great scarp, which forms the northern edge of the Knapdale Forest.

HOLY 'CILLES'

The northern part of this peninsula is congested with low-lying moorland hills, the lower flanks of which tend to be heavily forested, especially in the north western areas around Loch Coille Bharr, where the Forestry Commission has an information and interpretive centre. The Knapdale Forest is indeed one of the Forestry Commission's largest plantings in this area. But the seemingly impenetrable cover is crisscrossed by forest tracks and roads, old highways and byways and numerous ancient sites. For this area is virtually littered with antiquities — small ruined settlements, ancient mills, holy 'cilles' (the cells of priests and monks, many from Iona) and wells, carved stones and standing

stones. As one would expect in an area of such antiquity, folk tales and legends are rife.

Wherever you are in Knapdale, you are close to the sea: the western waters of the Gael. The west coast of the peninsula is heavily indented by great sea lochs, Loch Sween and Loch Caolisport, and the small rocky bays and inlets are a delight. The village of Tayvallich on Loch Sween is a good centre for those exploring the area, with a camping and caravan site as well as a hotel. There is much to be seen on the coastal roads, with

FORESTRY COMMISSION, EDINBURGH

▲*Dunardry walk takes you through the Knapdale Forest which contains both natural woodland plus conifers which are planted and harvested.*

many archeological sites of interest. At Kilmory near the Point of Knap, and at Keills where the road ends on the westerly point of the peninsula, and again at Eilean Mor, an island 2 miles (3.2 km) offshore from Kilmory, stand three ancient chapels dating from the 11th to the 14th century. These places are famous for their carved Celtic stones and crosses. Eilean Mor can be reached by hiring a motor boat at Crinan.

NORMAN STRONGHOLD

Some 2½ miles (4 km) north of Kilmory, close to the shore of Loch Sween, stands Scotland's earliest Norman stronghold. The squat, square building was built by Somerled between 1125 and 1135, while driving the Vikings from mainland Argyll. A keep and round tower were added to the building in the 13th and 14th centuries.

The highlight of this walk is the superb view from the top of Dunardry (the fort of Ardry) Ⓐ. This provides panoramas across the forest-covered 'knapps' of Knapdale towards the Isle of Jura to the south west, and across the strange flat Moine Mhor Ⓑ, The Great Moss, to the north towards the ancient rock of Dunadd Ⓒ, which is topped by the remains of a 5th-century fort. It was here that Fergus Mor MacErc of the tribe of Scotti in the Glens of Antrim came in 498 AD to be crowned King of Dalriada, the embryonic Kingdom of the Scots.

Tradition claims that Fergus was crowned seated upon the sacred 'Lia

▲The inner Hebridean island of Jura, south of the Mull, with its tiny population, can be seen from the walk.

STB/STILL MOVING PICTURE LIBRARY

Fail', or Stone of Destiny, that great slab of sandstone which was carried to this country from Ireland in fulfilment of an ancient prophesy. The prophesy claimed that where the stone rested the race of Scotia would prevail. Little is left of that once-royal shrine, only a carved footprint of fealty and an anointing stoup (a carved depression in the rock) alongside a faint outline of a wild boar, the totemic emblem of the tribe of Fergus Mor.

The return journey leaves the forest behind just west of Cairnbaan **D** and follows the towpath of the Crinan Canal **E**. This waterway, a popular route for yachts and fishing boats, cuts out an 80-mile (128-km) journey around the Mull of Kintyre. Opened in 1801, it connects Loch Gilp at Ardrishaig to the sea at Crinan on the Sound of Jura.

GHOSTLY FIGURES

The canal itself is 9 miles (14.4 km) in length and has 15 locks. Starting at the first sea lock at Ardrishaig it runs behind the village beyond the old chapel of Kilduskland where the ghostly figures of the White Friars are said to be occasionally seen gliding to and fro.

Beyond the first of the lock keepers' cottages at Miller's Bridge the canal approaches Cairnbaan, the site of an old drover's inn. Beyond the present hotel a waymarked trail climbs up the hillside to the Cairnbaan rock carvings, a series of huge, flat, natural slabs that are heavily decorated with prehistoric cup and ring markings.

The Forestry Commission

Twelve hundred of years ago the highlands of Scotland were covered in dense forest. These forests of Caledonian pine, birch and oak offered a sanctuary to bears, wolves and deer, and a hiding place for outlaws. The destruction of this Great Forest of Caledon began around AD 800 when it was burned by the Vikings, probably to smoke out their enemy, the Picts. A tremendous amount of timber was felled for boat and house building, and in following centuries the forests were burnt to rout out wolves, which plagued towns and their animal stocks.

Following a ban of tree felling to fuel iron smelters in England in 1584, the smelters moved to the highlands and proceeded to devastate the remaining areas of Caledonian forest. This destruction continued into the 19th century when lowland flockmasters set fire to the remaining areas of forest to give more space for their sheep.

The result was a vast shortage of timber during World War I, which led to the creation of the Forestry Commission. Established in 1919, the Commission's brief was to produce a timber reserve against any more national emergencies. This resulted in vast densely planted forests of Norwegian Sitka spruce.

The resulting work produced at the outbreak of World War II some 435,000 acres (176,000 hectares) of woodland. A White Paper report in 1943 proposed the establishment of a national forest of five million acres (two million hectares) by 2000. This target was in fact reached by 1983.

In the last couple of decades, however, the recreational potential of the forests has been highlighted and new plantings are considered with an eye on the effects on the landscape in addition to the effects on natural water courses. New grants to encourage the planting of native hardwood species have been forthcoming and the Commission itself now employs wildlife officers to record and encourage forest wildlife. An initial 46 Forest Nature Reserves, spread over the length and breadth of mainland Britain, have been chosen to represent the best of forest wildlife.

In addition to the management of woodlands throughout the country, thousands of miles of forest roads and tracks have been opened up to the public for recreational use.

FORESTRY COMMISSION, EDINBURGH

Managing the pine forests of Britain has changed radically over the years. Where the sweat of men once ruled, the chainsaw and the purpose-built forwarder (below) have taken over the woodlands.

FORESTRY COMMISSION, EDINBURGH

A riverside walk in the heart of Burns country

Although Alloway is now a suburb of Ayr, it has a long history as a separate village in its own right as well as many associations with its most famous son, Robert Burns. The poet was born in 1759 in a 'clay biggin', which has been preserved as one of the best surviving examples of traditional rural housing in the western Lowlands.

THE FAMILY HOME

The cottage **A** is single-storey and thatched, with walls of solid clay. It is protected from the weather by harling (a kind of roughcast) and whitewash and was designed to accommodate people at one end and livestock at the other. The living end is divided into two sections, the 'but' and the 'ben'. The former is the kitchen and communal living area and the latter the private sleeping

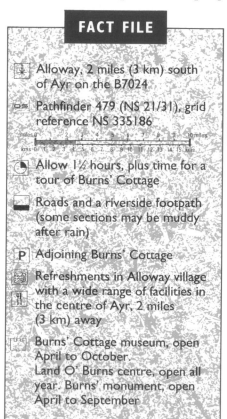

SCOTLAND IN FOCUS. INSET: E.A. JANES/NHPA

▲ In Burns' poem, Tam O'Shanter escaped from witches across Alloway's 13th-century Old Bridge of Doon. Honey fungus (left) grows on damp wood such as this fallen beech tree.

18th-century tombstones. Burns' father William (who used the old spelling of their surname – Burness) is buried here. The building, which was ruined in Burns' day, is best known for its association with one of his most famous poems, *Tam O'Shanter*. Riding home from Ayr in the midst of a storm, the

room, which would have been for the head of the family and his wife. The cottage contains period furniture, some of which belonged to the Burns family, and was supposedly built by the poet's father. Although it may seem crude by modern standards, it was quite a substantial and well-built dwelling in its day. Next door there is a small museum which contains an extensive collection of Burns' manuscripts and letters.

TAM O'SHANTER

Overlooking the valley of the River Doon stands the roofless shell of Alloway's historic old parish kirk **B**, surrounded by a fine collection of

▼ The cottage where the poet Robert Burns grew up was built by his father, who was an Ayrshire farmer.

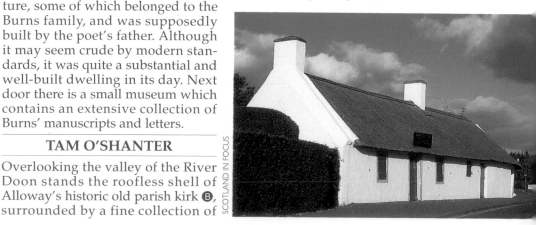

SCOTLAND IN FOCUS

THE WALK

ALLOWAY

*The walk begins outside Burns' Cottage **A** in the centre of Alloway.*

1 Follow the B7024 southwards to Alloway Kirk **B**. Almost opposite the church, a side road leads to the Land O' Burns Centre **C**. After visiting the centre, return to the main road.

2 Carry on towards the River Doon, but before reaching the river take a side road to the left to the Burns Monument **D**.

3 Carry on past the monument and cross the river by the Old Bridge of Doon **E**. Continue uphill until you rejoin the B7024. Turn right and recross the river by the New Bridge until you are back at Alloway Kirk.

4 A short distance beyond the church, turn left down a side road that leads to the river and continue downstream along the riverside path.

5 Climb uphill to reach the driveway to Cambusdoon House **F** and follow the road through a housing estate to a T-junction. Turn right and follow the road back to the B7024 and Burns' Cottage where the walk began.

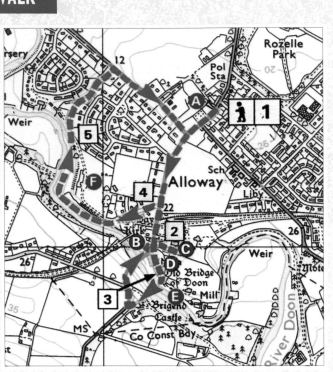

---

drunken Tam stumbled upon a gathering of witches among the ruins of the old church. He watched their revels until, taken by the dancing of a beautiful young witch, Nannie, he shouted out to encourage her and then had to gallop for his life with the witches in hot pursuit.

LIFE-SIZE STATUES

The Land O'Burns Centre **C**, which is open all year, contains a theatre where you can see a multi-screen presentation about the life and times of the poet as well as an exhibition concerning the places that are associated with him. Closer to the river is a monument **D** to the poet, erected in 1823. The garden in which it stands contains full-size statues of the incautious Tam and his drinking crony Souter Johnnie.

The River Doon is spanned by the Old Bridge **E**, a high-arched struc-

▼*The walk passes through the beautifully maintained gardens that surround the ruins of Cambusdoon.*

ture reputed to date from the 13th century. Today it is restricted to pedestrian traffic. In Burns' poem, when Tam was fleeing from the witches on Meg, his grey mare, he escaped by crossing the bridge over the river. His pursuers could not follow him across running water but Nannie, fleet of foot, was right on his heels and as Meg reached the keystone she grasped the horse's tail and pulled it off!

From the crest of the bridge there is a fine view of the famous 'banks and braes of bonnie Doon' that were immortalized by the poet. The woods on the far side of the river form part of the Doon estate where Robert's father once worked as a gardener. A short distance upstream are the remains of Brigend Castle.

CAMBUSDOON

From the New Bridge there is a good view of the steep-sided valley through which the River Doon runs its course. Further downstream and above the path are the ruins of Cambusdoon House **F**. The house was constructed for a local industrialist. When it was built in the early 19th-century, it was an imposing mansion of Scots-baronial style. The surrounding gardens and woods are still well maintained.

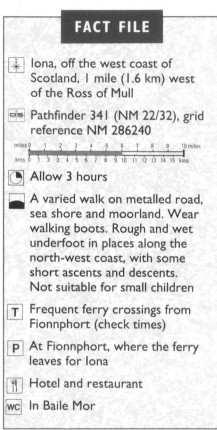

Hebrides' most splendid building, and to absorb the atmosphere of the place. Beautiful stone crosses stand in front of it, and inside the abbey complex are the reconstructed cloister and a bookshop. There is also a museum to be found here.

The exact site of St Columba's

FACT FILE

☀ Iona, off the west coast of Scotland, 1 mile (1.6 km) west of the Ross of Mull

⊡ Pathfinder 341 (NM 22/32), grid reference NM 286240

miles 0 1 2 3 4 5 6 7 8 9 10 miles
kms 0 1 2 3 4 5 6 7 8 9 10 11 12 13 14 15 kms

◔ Allow 3 hours

◖ A varied walk on metalled road, sea shore and moorland. Wear walking boots. Rough and wet underfoot in places along the north-west coast, with some short ascents and descents. Not suitable for small children

T Frequent ferry crossings from Fionnphort (check times)

P At Fionnphort, where the ferry leaves for Iona

🍽 Hotel and restaurant

wc In Baile Mor

▲ On the west side of the island, the walk passes some beautiful sandy coves. In summer plumage, the golden plover's gold-speckled upper parts contrast with its black belly (left). Baile Mor (right) is the only village on Iona. It is here that the jetty, where the ferry comes in from Mull, is to be found.

A walk around a beautiful island rich in Christian history

In the spring and early summer, the wealth of birds and abundant wild flowers make a walk on this tranquil island a delightful experience. Iona is a low, sandstone island, 3½ miles (5.6 km) long and 1½ miles (2.4 km) across. Within this small area lies a site of great importance for the history of Christianity.

Half a million visitors disembark at the jetty Ⓐ every year, many of whom are day trippers during the summer months, and venture no further than the church Ⓑ and the abbey Ⓒ. Farther afield, the walker will find peace and natural beauty in abundance, with an unspoilt coastline of shady beaches, rocky cliffs, undulating moorland and fine farmland where the traditional Hebridean crofting life continues untouched by the many visitors. It is well worth taking some time to explore the abbey, probably the

THE WALK

IONA

The walk starts from the jetty **A** *at St Ronan's Bay, where the ferry arrives from Fionnphort.*

1 On leaving the jetty, follow the road straight ahead, passing a sign on the right which points the way to the abbey. Follow the road to the nunnery and go through a gate into the nunnery grounds to see the remains. Continue through another gate to rejoin the road again; this leads you past the parish church **B**. After a few minutes' walk, you reach the abbey **C**.

2 After exploring the abbey, continue on the road northwards for about 15 minutes, until a track bears left to the farm of Lagandorain **D**. At this point there is a metal gate ahead and a sign 'Footpath to North Shore'. Go through the gate and follow a grassy track with a wire fence on the right. The Hill of the Seat **E** is now close by on the left. There is another metal gate and the track continues to the shore. A gate through the fence north of the Hill of the Seat gives access to the beach of Traigh an t-Suidhe **F**.

3 Follow the coast westwards from here, either by walking along the beach, or by following the grassy machair (boggy links land) above. After reaching

the western end of Traigh an t-Suidhe, the route continues along a rocky shoreline with low rocky hills to the left. Just before Carraig an Daimh **G** there is a fence which can be crossed at the seaward end where it reaches the rugged shore rocks. Here the coast becomes much steeper, with cliffs dropping to the sea and the sweep of round pebbles below Carraig an Daimh. Therefore from here it is necessary to walk up onto the undulating moorland above the sea. The path is indistinct, but there are several sheep tracks and it is easy enough to find a route which leads down again and comes to another fence. Where this joins a cliff, bypass it by descending a gully to the shore, walking round the base of a small cliff and ascending another gully. There is another ½ mile (800 metres) of similar terrain — moorland with rocky outcrops — until the route emerges on the machair at the northern end of Camus Cuil an t-Saimh **H**.

4 Having left the moorland behind, the going immediately becomes much easier on the smooth green grass sweeping round the back of the bay. Before reaching Camus Cuil an t-Saimh, there is a beautiful secluded sandy bay on the right, bounded by the islet of Eilean Didil **J**. Walk along the back of this bay and then cross a fence with a stile to reach the shore of the main bay. Follow a fence parallel to the shore for a little way until it swings left. Continue a little further on the same course, parallel to the shore, until a sandy track is reached, leading inland from the beach. This track leads to a metal gate, after which it becomes a tarmac road and crosses the island for almost 1 mile (1.6 km). Just as it comes close to the shore of the Sound of Iona, the road turns left and continues for another ½ mile (800 metres) to the jetty where the walk began.

original monastery is not known for certain, but many believe that the present abbey stands on it. In St Columba's day, the church and houses would have been built from wood and wattle, and surrounded by an earthwork vallum to mark the boundary and keep out cattle. The monks went out from Iona to found more monasteries and churches among the provinces of the Picts. Such was Columba's influence that, for a thousand years after his death, the island was known as 'I-Chaluim-cille' — the island of St Calum.

The road that the first part of this walk follows goes north, away from the area where most tourists gather, and passes several crofts, where sheep and cattle graze. Eventually the road reaches the grazing land at the north end of Iona, beyond Lagandorain **D**, the last farm. A small rocky knoll on the left is known locally as the Hill of the Seat **E** — it was reputedly a favourite spot visited by St Columba. Colourful lichens grow profusely on the rocks. Iona's geographical position ensures superb views of the

DEREK FORSS

◄*The dark-coloured, stone Maclean's cross can be found near the remains of the abbey and was built around the 15th century. The little island of Staffa (below) is famous for its rock formations, including Fingal's cave; it is visible from Iona.*

with the florally sterile tidal zone of shell-sand. This is followed by sand dunes where marram grass grows thinly on the seaward side and begins to stabilize the dunes. Gradually a rich shell-sand grassland is established, which is heavily grazed by crofters' stock.

HEBRIDEAN ISLAND

The flowers of the machair, offset by the blue of sea and sky, are a delight on a fine summer's day. There are dozens of species here such as harebell, primrose, wild pansy, wild thyme, bird's-foot trefoil, forget-me-not, eyebright, daisy and buttercup, as well as many others.

scattered islands of the Inner Hebrides — east to the rugged coast of Mull, west to Coll and Tiree and north to the Treshnish Islands: Rhum, Ulva and the basalt island of Staffa. The latter is the site of Fingal's Cave, made famous by the composer Mendelssohn in his Hebrides Overture after his visit to the region in 1829.

MACHAIR AND MOORLAND

The next stretch of the route is on machair and moorland along the north-west coast of Iona. Machair is the term given to the grassland that grows on shell sand along coasts in the Hebrides. The machair starts

NATIONAL TRUST FOR SCOTLAND, EDINBURGH

◄*The hay ricks on this piece of land near Ruanaich are evidence of the strong crofting traditions of Iona.*

Although Iona cannot rival islands such as St Kilda or Handa for the sheer spectacle of their huge sea-bird colonies, there is a wide variety of birds to be seen here, as on all Hebridean islands. They range from sea-birds to waders and the birds of the machair such as the golden plover and the skylark.

SANDY BEACH

Where the route heads west behind the sandy bay called Traigh an t-Suidhe ❺ (Strand of the Seat), the sandy beach also has many rocky outcrops and pools. The close-cropped machair is a delight to walk on but the going gets rougher and rockier beyond the western end of the bay. The machair abruptly changes to moorland vegetation

SCOTLAND IN FOCUS

Christianity on Iona

DEREK FORSS

Iona is of great importance to Christianity, although it was also used by Druids before the birth of Christ. St Columba landed here from Ireland in AD 563 and founded a monastery as a centre from which to convert the mainland Picts. He lived here until his death in AD 597, and under his influence Iona became the Christian centre of Europe.

There is strong evidence that the Book of Kells was written here. In the following centuries Norsemen raided the island, causing much death and destruction. The monastery was rebuilt in 1074 and again in 1203. A nunnery was also built at this time, and today the beautiful remains of pink granite are covered in grass and wild flowers. In 1500, the abbey

Iona's abbey is the feature that attracts most of the island's visitors. It was probably on this site that St Columba founded his monastery.

achieved cathedral status, but during the Reformation all the ecclesiastical buildings were dismantled and nearly all of the island's 350 crosses were destroyed. In 1549, it was recorded that 60 kings — Scottish, Irish and Norwegian — were buried near the site of the abbey, but their tombs have long since vanished.

The ruins of the abbey church were restored by 1910, and later the monastic buildings were also restored, by the Iona community, between 1938 and 1965. The island is now in the care of the National Trust for Scotland.

the islands of Coll and Tiree.

Eventually there is a beautiful view of the lush machair behind Camus Cuil an t-Saimh as the path descends from the moor onto smooth green grass sweeping round the bay. There are some fine sandy beaches tucked away between rocky headlands and islets such as Eilean Didil ❿. At this part of the walk, the main bay curves around to the hilly moorland at the south-west end of Iona. The machair is rimmed by a storm beach of thousands of smooth pebbles and rocks thrown up to the back of the beach by winter storms. At low tide there are many birds such as oystercatchers and sandpipers feeding on the shore.

THE CORNCRAKE

As you cross the island back to the Sound of Iona, you pass several crofts. In the summer, corncrake may be heard — but rarely seen — in the hay meadows. Though this bird was once common, it is now increasingly rare in the British Isles due to a loss of habitat caused by modern farming methods. It can, however, be found in places such as Iona where the traditional methods are still widely practised.

On reaching the eastern shore of the island, facing the Sound of Iona, the road turns northwards. It leads back to Baile Mor, passing several more crofts, scattered along the coast, as well as a war memorial and finally returns to the jetty.

▼*On Mull, across the Sound of Iona, the mighty Ben More stands at 3,169 feet (966 metres) above sea-level.*

which is boggy in some places.

The promontory of Carraig an Daimh ❼ forms a rocky hillock above an expanse of round pebbles and leads down to a small inlet known as Port Carraig an Daimh. Cattle graze on lush patches of grass amongst the rocks. Above, the steepness of the cliffs makes it necessary to walk inland a little way to cross the rough moorland between here and Camus Cuil an t-Saimh ❽ (Bay at the Back of the Ocean). Seals may be seen on the shore, and the lucky and observant visitor may even see an otter. Occasionally it is possible to see the Caledonia MacBrayne ferry as it runs backwards and forwards between

ALBA PICS

BEAUTIFUL BUTE

JOHN WATNEY

are the remains of an ale house **C**, which served the thirst of the crews of those ships. There is no road to the bay, so supplies must have been brought in by sea. Its well is now almost completely filled in.

POOL OF HEALING

The walk progresses along a wild, remote shore and involves a bit of scrambling. There is a series of sharp inlets, formed by fingers of rock with black grit beaches. The route continues to a ridge overlooking the beautiful Loch na Leighe **D** (The Pool of Healing). The edges are broadly rimmed with bulrushes; yellow water lilies and seabirds cover most of the surface. It is a lovely wildlife sanctuary. Sedge warblers occupy an island which is actually a mass of willow roots, and teal and tufted duck nest floating in the bulrushes. Stonechats, whinchats, pipits and wheatears can be

◀ *South of Kilchattan, the route follows a raised beach (one that, due to changes since its formation, lies above water level). Elderberries (below), which ripen in September, are used to make a wine.*

A craggy island coast and ancient remains

The woods at the south end of Kilchattan **A** give way to a raised beach with shoulder-high bracken and squelchy ground underfoot. On one side is an interesting rocky shoreline, on the other, shrub and bracken-covered cliff faces. As you head towards the lighthouse **B** at Rubh' an Eun, just over 1 mile (1.6 km) away, there are many geological phenomena to see.

SEMI-PRECIOUS STONES

These include columnar sandstone, honeycomb eroded red sandstone and carboniferous lava flows. The expert eye may discover in them linings of jasper, agate and garnet. There is a fine view from here over the Firth of Clyde, with yachts and commercial shipping making their

PAUL STERRY/NATURE PHOTOGRAPHERS LTD

way between Bute and the Great and Little Cumbrae Islands.

The lighthouse on the east arm of Glencallum Bay is a modest structure on a small plateau of big rounded pebbles. There is often a yacht or two anchored in the bay, a reminder that it was here that sailing ships out of Glasgow would drop anchor, while waiting for a favourable wind, before heading out into the Atlantic. Above the beach

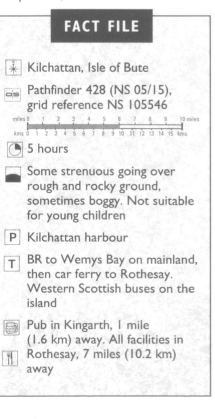

FACT FILE

✴ Kilchattan, Isle of Bute

🗺 Pathfinder 428 (NS 05/15), grid reference NS 105546

miles 0 1 2 3 4 5 6 7 8 9 10 miles
kms 0 1 2 3 4 5 6 7 8 9 10 11 12 13 14 15 kms

◔ 5 hours

▰ Some strenuous going over rough and rocky ground, sometimes boggy. Not suitable for young children

🅿 Kilchattan harbour

🚉 BR to Wemys Bay on mainland, then car ferry to Rothesay. Western Scottish buses on the island

🍴 Pub in Kingarth, 1 mile (1.6 km) away. All facilities in Rothesay, 7 miles (10.2 km) away

THE WALK

KILCHATTAN – ST BLANE'S HILL

The walk starts from the end of the houses to the south of Kilchattan village **A**.

1 ▶ Walk along the tree-shaded path beside the water. Emerging from the wood, go through a gate onto the broad, raised beach and follow in the footsteps of other walkers who have trodden down the bracken and grass. Stepping stones and crude duck boarding over the boggy stretches indicate the way. When the raised beach narrows and peters out, the worn track takes to the side of the cliffs. After passing several overhangs and a very narrow point, the track slopes down to the level pebbled area around the lighthouse **B**.

2 ▶ With the lighthouse behind you, pick a way over the boggy ground between hundreds of boulders, walking downhill to the beach at the head of Glencallum Bay. Walk inland off the beach for about 100 paces to look for the remains of the ale house **C** and its well. Return to the beach and walk up the right arm of the bay. A fairly discernible track that keeps close above the edge of the rocks leads to the next small bay, Boyd's Port.

3 ▶ When the east tip of this bay is in line with the distant lighthouse turn sharp right and look for an incline running left to right from the foreshore up the hillside. The path becomes a narrow stony sheep track, which climbs up to (and provides a trodden path through), a belt of heavy bracken. Finally you reach a narrow ridge looking down into the next bay. Walk diagonally down a fairly steep, grass slope to the rocky foreshore below. Pick your way round and over rocks and black beaches of three such inlets until reaching one with a large, rusty drum or boiler, lying above the waterline.

4 ▶ Turn inland and take a rock slope up to the right and then left. At the top follow a well-defined sheep run (confirmed by the droppings). This climbs diagonally uphill towards a saddle between two bumps in the ridge ahead. From the middle of the saddle, overlooking Loch na Leighe **D**, descend along another sheep track to the left side of the loch.

5 ▶ Skirt the loch, either along the raised bank running its length or by a worn track below and to the left of it, until you meet a tractor track. This leads to The Plan Farm. Continue round the house and at the T-junction with the farm road turn left downhill. Ignore a left-hand bend and walk directly across a field to a stone wall and a kissing gate.

6 ▶ Turn right through the gate and follow the stone wall uphill to the gate into the grounds of St Blane's Church **E**. Retrace your steps, but continue alongside the stone wall to the gate that leads to the turning circle at the end of the road from Kingarth.

7 ▶ From the gate walk up the road past Dunagoil farmhouse and through the metal gate on the left. The way from here to Dunagoil Bay is well worn, and signposted where it passes through a stone wall. On reaching the beach walk past the volcanic plug **F** with its small cave, then carry on round the end of the escarpment ahead to view the front of the fort **G** and its cave. A slope at the left-hand end of the escarpment provides a way up to the top. Return to the road.

8 ▶ From metal gate turn left to Lubas Farm, then downhill to Largizean and on past corner of the Suidhe Plantation, surrounded by a stone wall. The second gap in this wall is a farm track, 70 yards (64 metres) down which is a Celtic sun-circle **H** on the right. Go back along the road to the first gap in the wall. Turn left into plantation and follow bridlepath to Kilchattan. Turn right through village to the start of the walk.

most striking features is its enchanting setting. There are remains here too of the Celtic monastery founded by St Blane in AD 570 and the small Norman church built among the monastery's ruins 300 years after it had been sacked by the Vikings in AD 790. They occupy a hollow backed by a rock escarpment. Ash and elm growing around and within the walls lend the place a silvan air. As you look south, you will see the ground slope away, making a green corridor to the sea. The present ruins are largely 12th century with a fine example of a Norman arch, but there are numerous signs of earlier buildings belonging to the original

◄*Loch na Leigh is surrounded by bulrushes and yellow water lilies float on its surface. Many birds nest here.*

seen on the rocks and among the surrounding bracken. Occasionally sharp-eyed walkers may spot a kestrel or buzzard overhead.

The next site is St Blane's Church **E**, half hidden among trees at the top of a gentle slope. One of the

▼*By the remains of St Blane's church, built in the 12th century, is the men's burial chamber of an earlier monastery.*

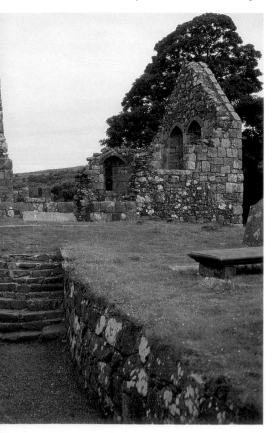

Nature Walk

As you walk along the beach you will find many interesting things washed up there, as well as in the sea itself. Look out for:

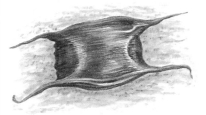

MERMAID'S PURSE You may occasionally see a young fish in this. It is actually the egg case of the dogfish, a kind of shark. These 'purses' are very common.

NAVIGATION BUOYS These are used to mark the channel for shipping. Black buoys mark the right, red ones the left and spherical buoys indicate shoals.

Just south of Dunagoil Bay are the remains of the vitrified Dunagoil fort, which dates back to the Iron Age.

monastery. These include two burial grounds (one for women and one for men), a corn-drying kiln, a stone basin where pilgrims washed their feet, a well, the lower remains of a tower and a long tombstone near the doorway to the burial ground traditionally believed to be that belonging to St Blane.

HIGH PROMONTORY

A short way ahead is Dunagoil Bay, where there is a volcanic plug **F**, a vitrified fort **G** and a cave. This is an excellent example of an Iron Age site. The fortification is partly natural (the precipice of a high promontory above the beach) and

◀*The last leg of the walk follows a bridle path through Suidhe Plantation, a pretty birch and oak wood.*

different shapes, still stand. The site is small but awesome — the stones have been standing there for 3,000 years. The last leg back into Kilchattan, a strung-out Victorian village of red sandstone, is by a pretty, though muddy, bridle path through a birch and oak wood that frames views of Kilchattan Bay with its scattering of yacht sails.

partly constructed (the wall at the top, of which little remains). There is not much to see, but a careful search will reveal lumps of half-melted vitreous stone which resembles slag from a furnace. The fort and the cave below were occupied for 300 years — the commanding location makes it an obvious defensive site.

▲*In the woods to the south of Kingarth there are three large standing stones — remains of a 3,000-year-old stone circle.*

Below it are caves, trap dykes of basalt thrusting through old red sandstone, columnar basal cliffs and pillow lava with steam cavities that give it the appearance of petrified sponge.

Further on there is a Celtic sun-circle ⊕, well hidden within a clearing of larch woodland. Of the circle, only three stones, of oddly

The Last of the Steamers

Four days a week during the summer, the passenger ship *Waverley*, the last seagoing paddle steamer in the world, steams into Rothesay harbour to pick up passengers for a round-the-island cruise. She is the last of the once great fleet of Clyde paddle steamers which, from 1890 to 1914, made Rothesay the Blackpool of the Clyde. In those years there were never fewer than 40 paddle steamers sailing the Firth, with a peak year in 1906 when their passenger load averaged some 60,000 every weekday of the summer.

The few steamers that had the nerve to move on Sundays were branded Sabbath Breakers. Even as late as 1920 sermons were preached in Rothesay against boats that sailed on Sundays. Until the outbreak of World War I, all the steamers provided bands and entertainments, the most popular being German bands playing Strauss waltzes. After the war there was less entertainment, although some newspapers sponsored pipe bands, highland dancing and firework displays. Since the 1940s, roll-on roll-off car ferries have provided a strictly utilitarian service and only *Waverley* is left to perpetuate the romance of the steamship era, though there are still tea dances in the Winter Garden at Rothesay.

At the turn of the century, the Firth of Clyde to the east of Bute was alive with paddle steamers packed with pleasure-seekers.

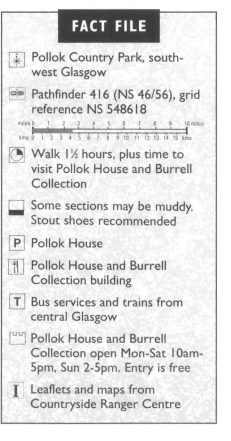

◀ *Town meets country at Pollok House which is only a few miles from Glasgow's centre. The three-spined stickleback (inset) is just one variety of fish found in the park's pond.*

A country house and gallery set in delightful woods and parkland

Glasgow is said to have more parks and open spaces than any other city in Europe. Among these is Pollok Country Park, the ancestral estate of the Maxwell family, which was given to the people of Glasgow in 1966. Full of character, it contains an extensive area of mature parkland and mixed woodlands — an enclave of rural peace where fallow deer roam a mere 3 miles (4.8km) from the centre of this bustling, friendly city.

The starting point of the walk is the car park by Pollok House, but your first port of call should be the Countryside Ranger Centre **A**, where useful pamphlets about the trees, birds and other wildlife can be obtained. This is not always open in the winter months however.

Next to the Ranger Centre is Old Stable Courtyard, the remains of a 19th-century farmstead, where owls, bats and starlings remain unmolested. About 70 Highland cattle, fierce-looking but placid, thrive on the field nearby.

DEMONSTRATION GARDEN

The neighbouring 2-acre (0.8-ha) demonstration garden **B** was established in 1975 in the original walled garden and is now used for educational purposes. Attractions include a garden for the disabled and an old gardener's bothy (hut), which has been restored to show what life was like for the gardener around the turn of the century.

Along the riverside, beside the yew trees, you may, if you are lucky, see a kingfisher; Glasgow is near the northern limit of their distribution. Mink and otters may also be spotted here on occasion.

After passing the tennis courts and main drive, you enter a wood of horse chestnuts, sycamores, limes and beeches that were planted about 100 years ago. Beyond this, in a modern building of imaginative design, is the Burrell Collection **C**.

SUPERB COLLECTION

This priceless collection of over 8,000 artefacts — textiles, ceramics, furniture, stained glass and works of art — was given to the city by shipping magnate Sir William Burrell in 1944. Ancient Chinese pottery is displayed alongside Japanese prints, Eastern tapestries and antiquities from Iraq, Egypt, Greece and Italy.

The main attraction on the rest of

FACT FILE

☀ Pollok Country Park, south-west Glasgow

▣ Pathfinder 416 (NS 46/56), grid reference NS 548618

miles 0 1 2 3 4 5 6 7 8 9 10 miles
kms 0 1 2 3 4 5 6 7 8 9 10 11 12 13 14 15 kms

◔ Walk 1½ hours, plus time to visit Pollok House and Burrell Collection

▭ Some sections may be muddy. Stout shoes recommended

P Pollok House

🍴 Pollok House and Burrell Collection building

T Bus services and trains from central Glasgow

🏰 Pollok House and Burrell Collection open Mon-Sat 10am-5pm, Sun 2-5pm. Entry is free

I Leaflets and maps from Countryside Ranger Centre

· THE WALK

POLLOK HOUSE – BURRELL COLLECTION

The walk begins at the car park next to Pollok House, at the southern end of the park.

▶ **1** Walk away from the house by White Cart Water, passing the Countryside Ranger Centre Ⓐ beside the Old Stable Courtyard. Continue along the road past the old weir and sawmill. You will see the demonstration garden Ⓑ on your left. The hard gravel road rejoins the river and passes through a strip of scrubland and an avenue of sycamores. On the left are a shinty field, a police-dog training centre and tennis courts where you emerge on Pollok Avenue, the main driveway, between two

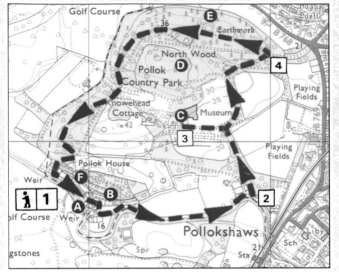

upright sleepers.

▶ **2** Turn left and cross the road. Walk up the path beside the road for about 60 yards (55m) until you see the Burrell Footpath signposted on your right beside a huge beech tree.

Follow this path through the chestnut trees. This section can become quite muddy. Follow signs to visit the Burrell Collection Ⓒ.

▶ **3** Turn left and go back along the road until the path forks off to the left

into North Wood Ⓓ. Proceed through a gate, past sycamores and elms, and turn right about 150 yards later. Keep right. You should see a waymarker sign on your left. Cross a bridge over a stream and the road beyond. You will see waymarkers ahead.

▶ **4** When you reach the tarmac driveway off Dumbreck Road, cross and turn left through the pine trees. You will pass a medieval motte Ⓔ on the right and later a fish-pond on the left. Follow the driveway as it bears left and crosses Lime Avenue near Lochinch Strathclyde Police Sports Club, crosses back again, and then rejoins it near Pollok House. Turn right to visit Pollok House Ⓕ and its precincts before returning to the car park.

---

the walk is varied woodland, full of birdlife. North Wood Ⓓ, a mature mixed woodland, covers the northern part of the park. The route leads through sycamores and elms and across a stream to an area of Corsican and Scots pines which

attract flocks of elusive coal tits. To the right of the path is a motte Ⓔ, typical of the kind built in the west of Scotland during the 12th and 13th centuries, although all that remains of it now are two round banks with a ditch in between. The banks would once have been the base of a stockade, within which the local people lived with their livestock.

ABUNDANT WILDLIFE

Further on is Pollok fish pond, which contains perch and three-spined sticklebacks, as well as frogs, toads and newts. If you are fortunate, you may see long-tailed tits chattering through the trees. There are also goldcrests.

Treecreepers, chiffchaffs and great spotted woodpeckers thrive on the old sessile oaks further along in the walk, while the red oaks and turkey oaks in the woods to the south abound with grey squirrels.

◀ *The peaceful woodlands of Pollok Park are a soothing antidote to the stresses of modern life. Imaginatively designed, the Burrell Collection (right) houses some 8,000 artefacts.*

A visit to historic Pollok House Ⓕ rounds off the walk through its 360-acre (145-ha) park. The neo-Palladian central block of the house, designed by William Adam, is probably Glasgow's most significant surviving piece of 18th-century domestic architecture, while inside is one of Britain's finest collections of Spanish masters, including works by El Greco, Goya and Murillo. There is also some superb 18th- and 19th-century furniture.

A stroll around a country town that is full of surprises

Probably nowhere in Scotland has so much of interest in one place as the little town of Biggar on the border of Clydesdale with Tweeddale. To make the walking as well as the seeing worthwhile, the route makes a circuit outside the town to take in some fine high-level views over the surrounding countryside and hills.

MEDIEVAL TOWN

Biggar is a medieval town that was created a free Burgh of Barony by James II in 1451 as a mark of favour to the local landowner, Lord Fleming. The town retains its

▶ *Cadger's Brig is thought to have been crossed by William Wallace in the 12th century, while he was spying on the English army. Selfheal (inset) grows in the grassland around Biggar.*

JOHN WATNEY. INSET: G.CAMBRIDGE/NHPA

FACT FILE

* Biggar, 25 miles (40km) south-west of Edinburgh

* Pathfinder 459 (NT 03/13), grid reference NT 038376

  miles 0 1 2 3 4 5 6 7 8 9 10 miles
  kms 0 1 2 3 4 5 6 7 8 9 10 11 12 13 14 15 kms

* Allow 5 hours to include visits to museums

* Pavements, lanes and roads

* P Car parks in High Street and Kirkstyle

* T There is a bus service from Lanark, which is served by trains to Glasgow

* Various cafés, restaurants, hotels, pubs and shops in Biggar

* WC Biggar Kirk Gillespie Centre

* I Tourist Information Centre open Easter to October, Tel. (01899) 21066. Albion Motors Archive, Tel. (01899) 21050

---

medieval layout, with a broad High Street designed to house a market. Most of the prominent buildings are Victorian, though a few date from the 17th and 18th centuries.

The walk begins at perhaps the oldest structure in the town, Cadger's Brig **A**, a bridge over Biggar Burn. Legend has it that in 1297 William Wallace crossed it disguised as a cadger, or pedlar, to spy on Edward I's army.

The bridge is on the way to the Gas Works **B**. The building, which dates from 1839, houses a small museum of early gas appliances, and the production of coal gas is explained by a video show.

MOAT PARK

It is just a short step to Burn Braes **C**, a grassy valley through which gurgles the little Biggar Burn. It incorporates Moat Park, with a play area that includes an exciting aerial ropeway. At one end of Burn Braes

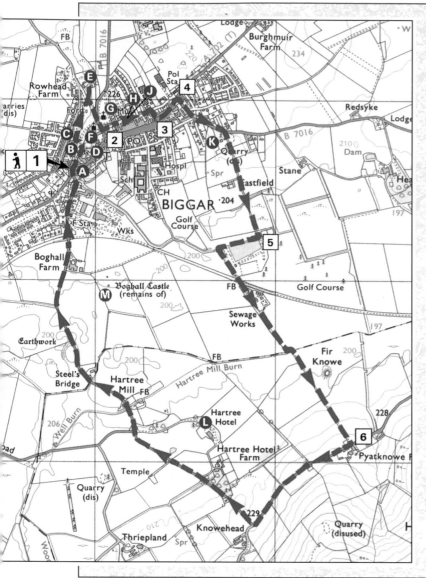

THE WALK

BIGGAR – HARTREE – BOGHALL CASTLE

The walk starts at Cadger's Brig Ⓐ behind the war memorial in Biggar.

▶ Walk up Gas Works Road to the Gas Works Ⓑ and museum. At the end of the road, take the path through Burn Braes Ⓒ, passing Motte Knowe Ⓓ on your right. At a road called Kirkstyle, turn left to leave an aerial ropeway on your left. Fork left down a steep, narrow road over a shallow ford to Biggar Mill car park, then cross a footbridge over the burn to Greenhill Farmhouse Ⓔ. Return to Kirkstyle and continue along it past Moat Park Heritage Centre Ⓕ on your right, then Old Kirk Ⓖ on your left.

▶ Turn left into North Back Road to Gladstone Court Museum Ⓗ and the Albion Motors Archive Ⓙ on your left. Turn right into Lambie's Close to reach the High Street.

▶ Turn left and continue walking for 300 yards (275m) to a crossroads by the police station.

▶ Turn right along a road signposted to Broughton. Take the third turning to the right to head down Park Road, signposted for the Puppet Theatre Ⓚ (on the right) and the Golf Club ahead.

▶ At the golf shop, turn right beside a boating pond, then left. Continue past a caravan park, over a footbridge, across dismantled railway lines, and straight on past the sewage works on your left. Beyond Fir Knowe, a small drumlin left by an Ice Age glacier, you reach a road by Pyatknowe Farm.

▶ Turn right. After ½ mile (800m), you come to a T-junction. Turn right up the lane (signposted to Biggar), and continue past Hartree Hotel Ⓛ and then the remains of Boghall Castle Ⓜ away to your right. The lane becomes Station Road, and ends opposite Cadger's Brig.

JOHN WATNEY

is Motte Knowe Ⓓ, a rounded hump that was the site of a Norman motte and bailey castle. At the other end is Greenhill Farmhouse Ⓔ, which now houses a museum, the subject of which is the Covenanters, the Presbyterians persecuted by the Crown in the 17th century.

HERITAGE CENTRE

Between the two is Moat Park Heritage Centre Ⓕ, which contains a fascinating and clearly-presented history of the region. Its models of crannogs, brochs and other ancient buildings are as good as, if not better than, those in more famous museums. Spitting Image has donated an image of the 18th-century

◀ *Biggar's old Gas Works, now open to visitors, has an interesting museum illustrating how gas was produced.*

ALL PHOTOS: JOHN WATNEY

◄Housed in the old works building is the Albion Motors Archive, where records and photographs have been kept of the company's fine old vehicles. In the Moat Park Heritage Centre, set up by the Biggar Museum Trust, this model of an ancient broch (below) is one of many exhibits that bring the history of the area to life.

political cartoonist, James Gillray, whose father was a local blacksmith.

On the opposite side of the road stands the Old Kirk **G**. The large 'through-stane', or tombstone, in the churchyard is marked with 150 years of Gladstone family names, ending with Thomas W Gladstone (died 1856), a cousin of the famous 19th-century Whig Prime Minister.

◄The stone-built Greenhill Farmhouse now contains a museum detailing the history of the Covenanters.

Just along North Back Road is the Gladstone Court Museum **H**, dedicated to the great man. This unusual memorial takes the form of a miniature street of Biggar shops and offices — a bank, a chemist, a shoemaker's, a dressmaker's and other tradesmen — reconstructed and stocked as they were in his day.

Perhaps the most fascinating exhibit in the museum is a 1900 Albion motor car, worth £40,000, which the Museum Trust bought in Honolulu. The car began its life in the Albion Motor Works, just behind Gladstone Court. The company was started in 1899 by Thomas Blackwood Murray with a capital of £1,300 raised by mortgaging the family farm. He is believed to have built the first British car made entirely by one man.

MOTORS ARCHIVE

Albion later became the largest lorry-building firm in the British Empire, but has since been absorbed by Leyland-Daf in Glasgow. Part of the old works is now the repository of the Albion Motors Archive **J**, with many thousands of photographs which may be inspected by prior arrangement.

The route makes its way out of the town past its most entertaining attraction, the International Purves Puppet Theatre **K**. A scaled-up version of the Victorian 'penny plain,

tuppence coloured' toy theatres, it boasts high-tech sound and lighting, and seating for over 100 people.

The puppets are illuminated by ultra-violet spotlights, and their bright costumes and painted features fluoresce on the darkened stage. There are matinees during most of the year, but seats must be booked in advance. Between shows, visitors are shown round a museum of antique puppets and taken backstage to meet the 'cast' and their puppet-masters.

Once you are out of the town, the walk heads through farmland where Aberdeen Angus cattle and

Clydesdale horses are bred. Further on, the lower slopes of the Hartree Hills give views back over the placid Upper Clyde Valley to Biggar and the hills beyond.

You return to Biggar along a quiet road. A short diversion up a drive leads to Hartree House ⓛ, a Grade II listed building in the Victorian Scottish Baronial style; parts of the house date back to the 15th century. It is now a country-house hotel, but non-residents are welcome to pass over the marble-paved threshold to admire the interior, whether or not they take a drink or a meal. The dining-room ceiling is a copy of that in Mary, Queen of Scots' bedroom in the Palace of Holyroodhouse in Edinburgh.

▶ *Where the route passes Pyatknowe Farm, there is a fine view over watermeadows to Broughton Heights.*

JOHN WATNEY

Working with Gas

NATIONAL MUSEUMS OF SCOTLAND

In the 1780s, the 9th Duke of Dundonald was heating coal to make tar when he realized that it was giving off an inflammable gas. He collected some of the gas in a retort and used it to fuel lights around his home. The first man to use gas commercially in Britain was also a Scot, William Murdoch (1754-1839). He installed a gas lighting system for the firm of Boulton and Watt, of James Watt fame, in Birmingham in 1798.

At first, gas works were custom-built for every private house or workshop using the fuel. The first supply piped to the public was installed in London in 1812 by the chartered Gas Light and Coke Company, formed by German-born Friedrich Winzer.

The Biggar Gas Works, opened in 1839, was among the pioneer suppliers of gas to small towns. Coal gas, or town gas as it was often called, was made by baking coal in sealed retorts of cast iron. The result had to be purified and scrubbed before it could be used, and the whole process produced useful by-products. Coke went to market-garden greenhouses, to large homes for central heating and to bakers to heat their ovens. Tar went to the Scottish Tar Distilleries, and ammonia to bleach makers. Whenever the purifiers were cleaned, local children with whooping cough were taken to the works to inhale the sulphur fumes, which were thought to have medicinal qualities. Gas manufacture ceased in Biggar on 4 January 1973.

This contemporary lithograph shows the Biggar Gas Works and the surrounding village houses as they were in 1873, 100 years before production ceased.

▼ *Built in the Scottish Baronial style, 1 mile (1.6km) to the south of Biggar, Hartree House is now a grand hotel.*

JOHN WATNEY

This country section of the walk twice crosses the border from Clydesdale into Tweeddale. Going from one to the other, the colour of the road changes from ochre to black. Soon after the second of these changes, and just before the boundaries of the town, is Boghall Farm. Behind the farmhouse, in a field, are the scant remains of medieval Boghall Castle ⓜ, the former home of Lord Fleming.

FOREST AND FALLS

21

G.THOMSON/SCOTLAND N FOCUS. INSET: W. LANKINEN/AQUILA

A woodland walk to a magnificent waterfall on the Isle of Arran

Arran is the most southerly of the Inner Hebrides. The shores of this quiet, unspoilt island, which is barely 40 miles (64km) from Glasgow, are washed by the Firth of Clyde. The island is sheltered from the Atlantic by the long arm of Kintyre, and warmed by the waters of the Gulf Stream.

This walk explores acres of forest, where the paths are bordered with summer flowers, on the way to a great gorge, a waterfall and a dramatic viewpoint of islands and mountains. It begins in the small coastal resort of Whiting Bay **Ⓐ**, whose houses straggle along the shore road. Once this was a fishing village; today it has the usual holiday attractions, a small art gallery and an 18-hole golf course.

Above the village there are quiet lanes **Ⓑ** edged with fuchsia, honeysuckle, pink campion and bush and kidney vetch. In the ditch beside the cart track that leads into the forest, forget-me-nots grow alongside orchids, marsh stitchwort, water mint, angelica, burdock and spearwort. Buzzards circle above, their keening filling the air.

FACT FILE

* Whiting Bay, Isle of Arran, 15 miles (24km) south of Brodick, on the A841

* Pathfinder 467 (NR 82/92/NS 02), grid reference NS 044261

* Allow 2-3 hours

* Some steady, but not too steep climbs. Woodland paths can be muddy after rain. Walking boots advisable

* **P** Car park opposite Old Pier Garage, Whiting Bay

* **⑪** Cafés in Whiting Bay

* **WC** Whiting Bay

▲*The view across the village of Whiting Bay to Holy Island, lying in the Firth of Clyde. The redpoll (inset) may be seen in the forest as you walk towards Glenashdale Falls (below). The falls' Gaelic name, Eas a' Chrannaig, means 'waterfall among trees'.*

A.G.FIRTH/SCOTLAND IN FOCUS

THE WALK

WHITING BAY – GLENASHDALE FALLS

The walk begins at the small car park opposite the garage and pier craft centre at Whiting Bay **A**.

1 ▶ Walk up the road above the car park. The road ascends steeply for about ¼ mile (400m), then ceases to be metalled as it passes through the buildings and greenhouses of Arran Nurseries.

2 ▶ Turn left at the lane **B** that skirts the golf course. At the crossroads, turn right, signposted to Glenashdale. After ½ mile (800m) the road is gated. Continue ahead on a cart track and through a gate into the forest **C**.

3 ▶ Cross a peat-stained stream by stepping stones and continue walking into the trees on a clear path until you reach a signpost pointing to the falls.

4 ▶ Turn left and walk along a reinforced path to the top of the Glenashdale Falls **D**. A railed area gives a very good view of the falls. Go back to the original track, turn left, and follow it as it bears right through the forest to a T-junction of paths.

5 ▶ Turn right, signposted to Lamlash. Follow this track, ignoring all turnings to the left, for about 1½ miles (2.4km). Where a signpost indicates Whiting Bay to the right, continue walking ahead to a picnic table on a grass verge in a clearing. The magnificent view **E** from here should not be missed.

6 ▶ Return to the turn-off to Whiting Bay, and descend through the forest. At the end of the path, turn right and follow a cart track that leads along the slope. Bear left downhill at a fork, and left again above and along Fairy Glen to the road at the seafront. Turn right to return to the starting point at the car park.

Once into the forest **C**, the path passes below ash, alder and birch and continues through plantations of Sitka spruce, the needles tinged with blue. The verges are vivid with banks of cross-leaved heath and mats of tormentil, which make a perfect colour foil. Goldcrests and coal tits chatter among the needles.

A glorious wooded glen contains the imposing Falls of Glenashdale **D**. They were formed when soft desert sandstone, which alternates with massive horizontal sills of harder rock, became eroded, over the years, by the Glenashdale Burn. The water now plunges 130 feet (39.6m) in two spectacular leaps into a densely forested gorge.

The walk continues through the forest to a magnificent viewpoint **E** over the sweep of Whiting Bay, with the romantically named Holy Island and its lighthouse lying across a narrow strip of silvery water. Out in the sound is Little Cumbrae. To the left are the stark granite peaks of the north of the island, often silhouetted against a dark blue sky.

From here, you make a gentle descent through the forest and the farmland which covers the lower slopes, to the evocatively named Fairy Glen, which leads you back into the village of Whiting Bay.

◀ *The remains of an Iron Age hill fort lie within the forest just off the route.*

THE FORGOTTEN GLEN

22

LOTHIAN

Through an area of outstanding beauty steeped in history

Roslin Glen is not only an area of dramatic scenery, but also a place intimately entwined in much of Scotland's turbulent past. During the last century, Roslin Glen was a popular venue for picnics and afternoon strolls, attracting many celebrities such as Scott, Wordsworth, Johnson and Burns. Further into the past it was a place where noblemen built castles, such as Rosslyn (after the family, in spite of Ordnance Survey's variations) Castle ⓛ. Armies mustered prior to battle, groups of rebellious young men sought refuge from the occupying English, and John Knox preached from a rocky pinnacle across the rippling waters of the River North Esk.

FACT FILE

⚹ Roslin, 9 miles (14.4 km) south of Edinburgh

⌖ Pathfinder 420 (NT 26136), grid reference NT 272632

miles 0 1 2 3 4 5 6 7 8 9 10 miles
kms 0 1 2 3 4 5 6 7 8 9 10 11 12 13 14 15 kms

◔ Allow at least 4 hours

⛰ There are paths along the entire route but it can be very muddy in places, especially in Bilston Woods. The path through Roslin Glen is eroded in parts and sometimes narrow where it clings to rocky crags. It can be slippery in wet weather

ⓟ In Roslin village; small car park near Rosslyn Chapel

ⓣ Frequent bus service from Edinburgh

🍴 Tea room at Rosslyn Chapel (summer only), two pubs serving light refreshments all day in Roslin. Toilets for patrons at all three places

GLYN SATTERLEY. INSET: ROGER TIDMAN/NATURE PHOTOGRAPHERS LTD

This circular walk across the plateau above the glen to Bilston Woods, returning through Roslin Glen itself, includes many sites of great historical interest, including Rosslyn Chapel ⓜ. Furthermore, the area around Bilston Burn and the woodland south-east of Roslin are Sites of Special Scientific Interest.

The walk begins in the delightful village of Roslin ⒜, which is known to have existed as a flourishing market town for over a thousand years.

BLOODY BATTLE

Just beyond Roslin to the north the skyline is dominated by the Pentland Hills with Dryden Tower ⒝ in the foreground. Dryden Tower was built in the 19th century by a

▲ *Roslin Glen is an Area of Outstanding Natural Beauty. The rare red squirrel (inset) can still be seen in these parts. The peaceful River North Esk (below) meanders through a battle site.*

GLYN SATTERLEY

THE WALK

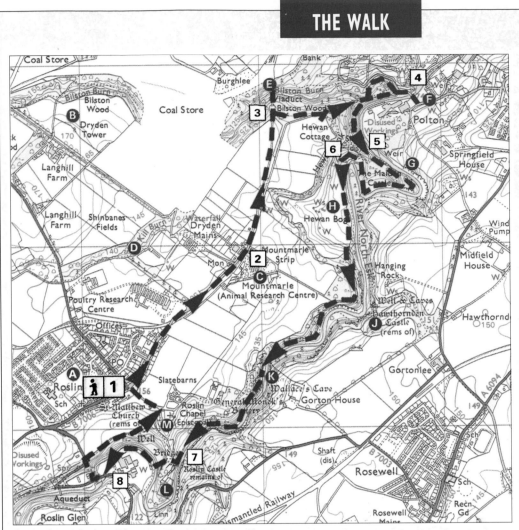

ROSLIN – POLTON

The walk begins at the war memorial next to the cross-roads in Roslin village **A**.

1 Leave Roslin along Manse Road. Shortly after leaving the stone cottages behind, the road crosses a disused railway bridge then passes between a 'No Through Road' sign and a sign for 'Dryden — Mountmarle Farm'. Dryden Tower **B** is to the left and, in the distance, the Pentland Hills. Do not veer off to the right over the old railway but continue to Mountmarle Farm Animal Research Centre **C**. Kill Burn **D** is to the left.

2 Keep strictly to the road through Mountmarle Farm and leave by the gravel road that runs beside a dismantled railway track. Shortly after the road passes through a cutting in the railway embankment, turn left on to the railway track and follow it as far as Bilston Viaduct **E**. Note that this track can be muddy. If it proves impassable, use the farm road to the right.

3 Turn back along the track for about 100 yards (90 metres) then descend left into Bilston Woods. Take the path near the edge of the woods. On reaching a gravel road turn left, pass a wooden gate and stile on the right, then follow the path as it curves left back into the woods and descends steeply into the depths of Bilston Glen. At the bottom of the glen cross a bridge, which can be very muddy, over Bilston Burn to reach an asphalt road. Follow this downhill to the River North Esk in Polton village **F**.

4 Retrace your steps along the road for 55 yards (50 metres), pass through a gap in the stone wall, climb the wooden steps ahead and follow the path along the knife-edge ridge between the North Esk and Bilston Burn. Far below are the remains of Polton Mill, one of many paper mills that once flourished along this river. Rejoin the path, continue, then turn left and walk across rough grass-land along the top of a cliff above the North Esk. Follow another narrow ridge and finally descend a steep path through gorse bushes to a junction of paths.

5 Ahead is Maiden's Castle **G**. Take the path to the left, above the weir, to the water's edge. Surrounded by sandstone cliffs, this is a fine spot for a rest or a picnic. Retrace your steps, but keep to the left to reach the junction of paths.

6 From here the route follows the river past Hewan Bog **H** and through Roslin Glen for about 2 miles (3.2 km) to Rosslyn Castle **C**. The path is never far from the river and there are several forks, but the paths ultimately rejoin. Soon after entering the woods, near the top of a long ascent, Hawthornden Castle **J** can be seen between the trees on the far side of the glen. Wallace's Cave **K** is a little further upstream, best seen from the path that leads to the water's edge.

7 At Rosslyn Castle, pass through the high archway, bear left around the base of the castle and cross the footbridge over the river. Continue upstream, skirting an area now used as a car park. This was once the site of an internationally renowned carpet factory and before that, during the Middle Ages, a linen bleach field.

8 Use the road bridge to cross the river once more, then immediately turn right along a path beside drainage works and climb to the higher road. Follow the railings along the road for a few paces then turn right on to a footpath high above the river, near a cemetery. Join the road coming up from the castle and continue uphill to a T-junction. To the right is Rosslyn Chapel **M**. Turn left to return to Roslin.

▼ *Bilston Viaduct, which spans Bilston Glen, was built to extend the railway from Loanhead to Roslin.*

▲ *Hawthornden Castle enhances the romantic atmosphere of Roslin Glen. The spectacular sandstone cliffs (below) are reached from the ridge path, described by Sir Walter Scott as 'one of the finest walks in the country'.*

and a local burn, later named Kill Burn ◗, is said to have run red with blood for three days.

CASTLES AND CAVERNS

Further along the route Bilston Viaduct ◗ is an impressive example of Victorian engineering built for the railway. The descent through Bilston Woods leads down into the Esk Valley and the village of Polton ◗, the home of Thomas de Quincey, a 19th-century poet known for his

local shipowner in order that he might spy his vessels approaching in the Firth of Forth.

The route passes through the rolling agricultural land of Mountmarle Farm ◗ , now an Animal Research Centre. Looking at these peaceful fields, it is hard to believe that one of Scotland's biggest battles occurred here. On 24th February 1302, Edward I's army of 30,000 Englishmen, brought north to subdue the rebellious Scots, were

finally beaten by 8,000 Scots.

The fighting raged throughout the glen, some of the worst slaughter occurring in Hewan Bog ◗ whose name derives from the 'hewing down' of the English. Many more English soldiers fled into the glen, and in the faint light of dawn tumbled over the waterfall beneath the castle and perished in the waters of the North Esk. So violent was the conflict that corpses were piled high and left to rot in surrounding fields

Nature walk

BADGER SETT Badgers are mainly nocturnal. During daylight hours they stay underground in tunnel systems called setts.

STRIPPED BARK Like other rodents, squirrels gnaw at timber and may strip bark from the branches of trees.

famous poem *Confessions of an English Opium Eater*. From Polton the path climbs over a dramatic, knife-edge ridge then descends to Maiden's Castle **G**. This is not, as you might expect, the site of an ancient castle, but a small hill, covered with trees, surrounded by the North Esk and sandstone cliffs. Local myth tells of a fairy queen who once lived at this scenic place.

The return journey is through the beautiful Roslin Glen following the River North Esk. Roe deer or badger may be glimpsed, or a heron skimming above the turbulent waters. Here too is Hawthornden Castle **J** built in the 15th century by the Drummond family and home of the poet William Drummond (1585–1649). Caverns beneath the castle and caves along the ravine have pro-

vided refuge to many throughout the ages. It was in Hawthornden caverns, in hiding from the English, that Robert the Bruce is believed to have encountered the famous spider which so influenced his military strategies. In a cavern large enough to hold 60 people, Wallace's Cave **K**, Sir William Wallace, a champion of Scotland's independence, spent five days in refuge.

Rosslyn Castle and Chapel

At Rosslyn Castle Edward I and his English forces were defeated in the 14th century by the Scots, led by Robert the Bruce.

'apprentice pillar'. Sir William ordered a Roman design for the chapel pillars and sent his master stonemason to Italy to seek instruction. In the mason's absence an apprentice undertook the task of carving such a pillar. He succeeded, which so enraged the master on his return that he lifted a hammer and killed the novice within the chapel walls, or so the story goes.

Rosslyn Castle stands on a pinnacle of solid rock surrounded on three sides by the North Esk River. Built in the 13th century by the St Clair family, the castle has frequently been battered and almost destroyed by war (and once by a fire started accidentally by a maid while searching beneath a bed with a candle for one of her Ladyship's puppies). It still remains in the hands of the St Clair family. The high Norman arch, which supported the only access to the castle, has recently been restored, as has the interior, and much of the wall and gate survive.

In 1450, William St Clair instigated the building of a great collegiate church in the shape of a crucifix on a hill near his castle. Unfortunately the building was never completed, but the top of the cross survives as the magnificent Rosslyn Chapel. Considered to be one of the finest of such buildings in Scotland, its elaborate stonework has earned the building an international reputation. It contains several intricately carved stone pillars, including the beautiful

ALL PHOTOS GLYN SATTERLY

Rosslyn Chapel is renowned for its ornamental carved stonework. Its dramatic exterior is complemented by the splendour of the interior, particularly the pillars. Built in the 15th century and fully restored, it is reputed to be one of the most beautiful chapels in Scotland.

GLYN SATTERLEY. INSET: M. READ/SWIFT PICTURE LIBRARY

Through the valley of the River Tyne and up Traprain Law hill

This walk through rural East Lothian follows a route past farmhouses and a grain mill to the ruins of Hailes Castle **E** on the banks of the River Tyne. The longer version leads up the grassy hillside of Traprain Law **D**.

PRESTON MILL

The walk begins near Preston Mill **A**, which is one of the few grain mills left in Scotland. Before the 18th century, small water-powered mills were scattered through the Scottish countryside. Each proprietor had the right of thirlage: the power to compel his tenants to grind their corn at his own estate mill. Thirlage

---

FACT FILE

* Preston Mill, off the A1 near East Linton, between Edinburgh and Dunbar

OS Pathfinder 408 (NT 47/57), grid reference NT 594777

| miles 0 | 1 | 2 | 3 | 4 | 5 | 6 | 7 | 8 | 9 | 10 miles |
| kms 0 | 1 2 3 | 4 5 | 6 7 | 8 | 9 10 11 | 12 13 14 15 | kms |

⏱ 4-5 hours, including visits to Preston Mill and Hailes Castle

▭ Country lanes, farm tracks and footpaths

P National Trust for Scotland car park beside Preston Mill

🍴 Cafés, shops and several hotels in nearby East Linton

I Preston Mill open 1 Apr–30 Sept. Admission ticket includes visit to dovecote on request

---

▲Hailes Castle belonged to the Earl of Bothwell who, it is said, married Mary, Queen of Scots. The lapwing (inset) ate soil pests after ploughing, but it has left farmland due to insecticides.

was gradually abolished and milling became a more commercial business. Preston Mill, which probably dates from the 17th or early 18th century, was powered by water from the nearby River Tyne.

RIVER FLOODS

The Tyne could be a fickle friend, however, as the levels of former floods marked on the walls of the mill testify. The curiously-shaped corn drying kilns beside the mill were vital because the harvest was frequently gathered late and wet.

There is an area south of Preston Mill where much of the old rural landscape of East Lothian was

THE WALK

turn right at the road junction beside Traprain Farm and continue along a road that descends back into the valley past Kippielaw Farm to rejoin the route at Stage 6. Follow the instructions from Stage 6 to return to the start. For the longer walk that takes in Traprain Law **D**, turn left at Traprain Farm.

4 Pass Sunnyside Farm, turn right at the junction and follow the road that skirts the north side of Traprain Law. Once you have passed the quarry at the eastern end of the hill, climb the steep grassy slopes to the summit. Return to the road and continue westwards for about 500 yards (450 metres) beyond the hill.

5 Turn right along the narrow winding track that leads downhill. At the T-junction turn left for about 500 yards (450 metres) to reach Hailes Castle **E**. Retrace your steps to the T-junction. Follow the track to the next T-junction (Stage 6).

6 Keep straight ahead down the valley into East Linton. Walk through the centre of East Linton and turn right on the B1407 to return to Preston Mill.

PRESTON MILL – TRAPRAIN LAW

*The walk begins near Preston Mill **A**.*

1 To visit Preston Mill cross the River Tyne by a footbridge. Retrace your steps and continue past the dovecote **B** through the yard at Phantassie Farm **C** to reach the main road.

2 Turn right along the main road (B1377) and follow it into East Linton. Turn left under the railway bridge, cross the A1, then turn left on a minor road that climbs up the side of the valley.

3 For the shorter walk,

swept away in the 18th and 19th centuries. But one common feature that typifies the old order is the doocot, or dovecote, a stone structure lined with hundreds of stone nest boxes. Like mills, doocots, such as Phantassie Doocot **B**, were owned by landowners – indeed most estates had one. (Pigeons were a valued source of fresh meat in winter and their droppings were highly prized as manure.) To have a look inside the doocot, ask a guide at Preston Mill, but be prepared for the smell when you get there!

Further along the route is Phantassie Farm **C** with farm buildings built around 1840. During the Agricultural Revolution many East Lothian farmsteads were rebuilt twice: first during the late 18th century in a solid but traditional style, then again in the mid-19th century with much greater pretensions. The

▶ *Preston Mill, a water-powered grain mill, is maintained by the National Trust for Scotland.*

ALL PHOTOS GLYN SATTERLEY

▲ *The mid tower in Hailes Castle which has been greatly altered since the 14th century and last used as a dovecote.*

19th-century farmsteads were designed by architects and laid out around a series of courts for maximum shelter and efficiency. Other farms in this area incorporated imitation gothic features: Sunnyside Farm looks like a medieval castle.

An important influence on farmstead layout began at Phantassie where Andrew Meikle, a local millwright, perfected the first effective corn threshing machine during the 1780s. Most early threshing machines were driven by horse power with the animals walking in a continuous circuit. Water and wind power were also used for driving threshing machines.

STEAM POWER

In the early 19th century, when better roads made the carriage of coal from mines in the west of the county easier and cheaper, many of the larger East Lothian farms converted to steam power for threshing. Engine houses and tall brick chimneys rose above the farm buildings. Seen from a distance these chimneys make the farmsteads seem like factories, which in a sense they were. Although some steam-engine chimneys have been demolished for safety reasons in recent years, many of them survive.

On the Tyne stands Hailes Castle, the most secluded of East Lothian's great medieval castles, hidden in the deep-cut river valley. Its site is a strong one though, overlooking a steep drop to the river on the north and protected by a ravine on the west and south. The earliest fortification on this site was probably a small stone manor house built in the 13th century. In the following century this was extended into a full curtain-wall castle with a roughly rectangular layout.

CASTLE RUINS

The remains that are visible today consist mainly of the northern part of the curtain wall linking two towers. Traces of other buildings within the courtyard of the castle can be seen, but the walls on the south side have been largely demolished — the

▶ *A Scotsman's home is his castle: Sunnyside Farm, situated on some of the most fertile farmland in Scotland.*

work of Oliver Cromwell's forces in 1650. Hailes Castle is now open to the public.

The full length of the walk takes in Traprain Law, a hill that dominates the valley of the River Tyne near East Linton. The hill is a dome of volcanic lava that was intruded between layers of other rocks far below the surface and has now been exposed by prolonged erosion. The hill is particularly steep to the south where there is a line of crags popular with rock climbers.

On the northern side, however, the grassy slopes allow an easy scramble. It is well worth the climb to the summit because there is a magnificent view across the valley, over East Lothian, the Firth of Forth, and the long blue line of the Lammermuir Hills to the south.

It was doubtless because of this superb vantage point that Traprain Law was chosen as the site for a small fort in late Bronze Age times. It enclosed an area of about 10 acres (4 hectares) close to the summit. Around 700 BC a more substantial stone rampart was constructed, taking in an area nearly twice as large. The fort was enlarged again, reaching its maximum extent of

▼ *Traprain Law (seen from Sunnyside Farm) where Roman silver was discovered.*

The Agricultural Revolution

The view from Traprain Law during the 17th or early 18th centuries would have looked very different from that of today. Instead of the modern pattern of large, regular fields bounded by hedges and stone walls, there was a patchwork landscape with unenclosed cultivated land divided into separate strips, separated by moorland and pasture.

By the 18th century, landowners began schemes of afforestation and began to enclose farms and tenant holdings. Yet by the mid-18th century, less than a quarter of the lowlands of East Lothian had been enclosed and improved. It took another 50 years for the 'real' Agricultural Revolution to arrive. Enclosure became universal here as the areas of common pasture were divided out and ploughed up. Small lochs and marshy hollows were drained and cultivated. The result was a highly efficient 'factory-farming' system.

William Cobbett, the celebrated English writer on agriculture and rural life, visited East Lothian in the 19th century and was impressed by what he saw. Many steadings have been rebuilt, but the countryside today is still very much the handiwork of the landlords of the 18th century.

A 17th-century engraving illustrating a landscape of enclosed fields.

MANSELL COLLECTION

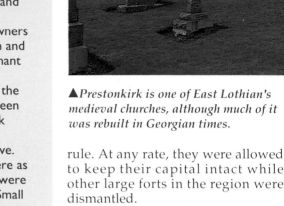

▲*Prestonkirk is one of East Lothian's medieval churches, although much of it was rebuilt in Georgian times.*

rule. At any rate, they were allowed to keep their capital intact while other large forts in the region were dismantled.

The fort continued in use into late Roman times. In 1919 a large hoard of Roman silver was discovered beneath the foundations of one of the huts. The silver included plates, bowls and other vessels which had been flattened and cut up as if ready for smelting. It may have been some kind of payment to a native chief either for providing troops to help guard the frontier or to keep him loyal to the Romans.

PRESTONKIRK

At the end of the walk, on the outskirts of East Linton, is the parish church of Prestonkirk. The greater part of the structure is a plain Georgian rebuilding from 1770, but a magnificent 13th-century chancel has survived from the earlier church – the best example of its kind in the Lothians. The churchyard has some attractive tombstones from the 18th century as well as the grave of Andrew Meikle, the inventor of the threshing machine.

East Linton's Jubilee Clock in the village square has been called Jessie's clock for over 100 years after a butcher's daughter, Jessie, who used to wait for her sweetheart beneath it.

◀*The view from the top of Traprain Law takes in East Linton, Bass Rock and the Firth of Forth.*

approximately 42 acres (17 hectares) in the first century AD. This made it the largest Iron Age fort in southeast Scotland.

The remains of the fort are so large that it is difficult to get a good view of it, but the ramparts are still clearly visible in many places. Excavations have shown that it was a densely built-up settlement, almost a town, with regular streets of buildings and a large permanent population.

ROMAN SILVER

The fort was the capital of a tribe known to the Romans as the Votadini and when the legions annexed southern Scotland the Votadini seem to have placed themselves voluntarily under Roman

24

SCOTLAND IN FOCUS. INSET: D. BRIGHT/SWIFT PICTURE LIBRARY

LOTHIAN

A short walk up the most northerly hill of the Pentland range

The major attraction of this walk is the tremendous views obtainable from virtually the entire route. Right from the start, as you rise up the steep sides of Caerketton Hill, the vista of Edinburgh and the rolling farmlands of Midlothian gradually unfold.

From the top of Caerketton Hill **Ⓐ** one can see the Moorfoot Hills, the whole of Edinburgh and clear across the Firth of Forth to Fife. But the most extensive views are from Allermuir Hill **Ⓑ**.

EXTENSIVE VIEWS

A viewfinder here helps identify the major topographical features in the vista below. To the east is the Bass Rock and the open sea, to the southwest the misty tops of the Pentland Hills and to the northwest the Forth Bridges and the Ochil Hills. In winter, when the air is crisp and clear, it is even possible to see Ben Lomond

▲*The wide sprawl of Edinburgh and Caerketton Hill can be seen from the top of Byreside Hill. The painted lady butterfly (inset) migrates from southern Europe and North Africa to Britain.*

mountain 60 miles (96 km) away.

On the descent you will pass Swanston **Ⓒ**, summer home of the young Robert Louis Stevenson, author of such classics as *Kidnapped*, *Treasure Island* and *The Strange Case of Dr Jekyll and Mr Hyde*. This picturesque hamlet seems almost untouched by time, white-washed cottages with thatched roofs and colourful gardens surround a village green through which trickles the Swanston Burn.

Stevenson loved Swanston and the Pentland Hills. The Swanston school house and farm can be recog-

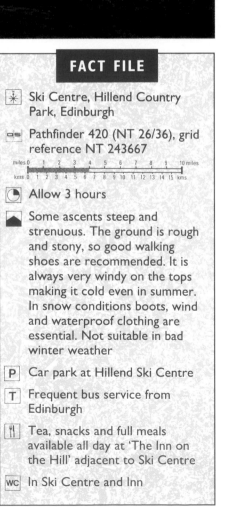

FACT FILE

✳ Ski Centre, Hillend Country Park, Edinburgh

🗺 Pathfinder 420 (NT 26/36), grid reference NT 243667

miles 0 1 2 3 4 5 6 7 8 9 10 miles
kms 0 1 2 3 4 5 6 7 8 9 10 11 12 13 14 15 kms

◖ Allow 3 hours

▲ Some ascents steep and strenuous. The ground is rough and stony, so good walking shoes are recommended. It is always very windy on the tops making it cold even in summer. In snow conditions boots, wind and waterproof clothing are essential. Not suitable in bad winter weather

Ⓟ Car park at Hillend Ski Centre

Ⓣ Frequent bus service from Edinburgh

🍴 Tea, snacks and full meals available all day at 'The Inn on the Hill' adjacent to Ski Centre

wc In Ski Centre and Inn

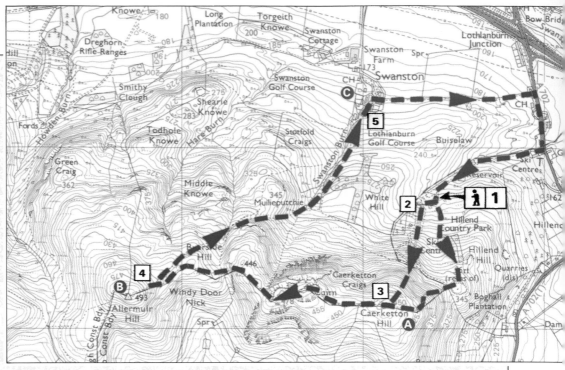

THE WALK

HILLEND – CAERKETTON HILL

This walk begins at the Hillend Ski Centre on the Pentland Hills just to the south of Edinburgh.

1 From the entrance to the fenced car park climb the grassy slopes to the left of the ski runs, heading slowly towards the line of small rocky hills. The path veers left at first, then climbs roughly parallel to the ski runs until you reach the highest of these small hills. Here you will find an Iron Age fort surrounded by remnants of defensive ditches. There is also a bench ideally sited for admiring the view. Climb the right-hand stile of the two that cross the fence behind the fort and follow the steeply rising path through the heather, joining a fence for the final ascent to a large cairn on the summit of Caerketton Hill **A**. From here to Allermuir Hill you will almost certainly be heading into a strong and probably very chilling wind. If you feel you are not prepared for this, turn back now.

2 As an interesting alternative you could, for a small fee, take the chairlift to the top of the ski slopes then cross the nearby stile and follow the path ahead up the steep side of Caerketton to the summit

cairn. Do not use the lift if you are too unfit to make the climb or you may discover later that you cannot complete the walk.

3 Head off along the stony path that follows a fence westwards down a little then up to a cairn above Caerketton Craigs. Do not wander too close to the edge here as it is a long drop down. Continue along the path beside the fence down into a gully then over the smaller Byerside Hill and on up to the summit of Allermuir Hill **B**. The summit of Allermuir Hill is unmistakable. It is the highest hill around and on top there is a triangulation pillar with a viewfinder on a second pillar.

4 Retrace your steps

down the final steep slope, then follow the path which forks left just before a tiny cairn of pink stones. This path passes a little to the left of Byerside Hill, crosses a burn running down from the right-hand end of Caerketton Craigs then forks. Take the right-hand path passing over a small saddle immediately beneath a craggy outcrop, then descend steeply into the gully of the Swanston Burn. Behind are the great scree slopes and ragged cliffs of Caerketton Craigs. Ahead is the T-wood (actually more like the shape of a crucifix). Fork right at the waymark post with the yellow arrows and follow the left bank of the burn. Shortly after passing beneath the boughs of a huge beech tree, you cross

to the other side and continue down right bank.

5 Enter the village of Swanston **C** through a swing gate and pass quietly along the asphalt road across the village green. Note the old schoolhouse, the last and largest of the white-walled buildings on the left. Follow the road round to the right, past a post box in the wall and some grey stone, terraced cottages then pass through the swing gate directly ahead and follow the signposted right-of-way along the bottom of Lothianburn Golf Course. After just over ½ mile (0.9 km) you will emerge onto a busy main road. Turn right, walk up to the entrance to Hillend park and follow the park road back to the Ski Centre.

nized in many of his novels and of the views from Caerketton he wrote with great affection: 'You look over a great expanse of champaign sloping to the sea… So you sit, like Jupiter on Olympus, and look down from afar upon men's life.'

◄*Swanston was the young Robert Louis Stevenson's summer home. He would have appreciated the stark landscape of Allermuir Hill (right), even in winter.*

BOTH PHOTOS: SCOTLAND IN FOCUS

25

LOTHIAN

GLYN SATTERLEY. INSET: STEPHEN DALTON/NHPA

▲ *Whereas once it was a busy link between Edinburgh and Glasgow, the Union Canal is now a peaceful place. The swallow (left) rarely alights on the ground and drinks on the wing.*

A country walk by canal, river and old railway in the heart of Edinburgh

The Water of Leith **A** flows from the Pentland Hills of the Firth of Forth through central Edinburgh. Its walkway forms one of the finest riverside walks in the country. Especially beautiful are the woodland sections, where the river runs through Craiglockhart Dell **B**, and the Gorge of Colinton Dell **E**. The mostly planted woods exhibit a tremendous variety of trees. In early summer, the smell of wild garlic here can be intoxicating. In former days, the river's power was used to drive water mills such as those at Redhall and beside Spylaw House **H**. The weir and lade (mill-stream) that supplied water to Redhall Mill **D** can still be seen and there are other weirs above Spylaw House and at Slateford **C**.

RURAL COMMUNITY

Colinton **G**, whose name means 'the village in the wood', was originally an isolated rural community that grew up around the head of Colinton Dell at a place that was easily forded by herdsmen and other travellers. It is now part of the city of Edinburgh, but has retained an authentic village quality with a

FACT FILE

✱ 2 miles (3.2 km) south-west of centre of Edinburgh on A70

🗺 Pathfinders 420 (NT 26/36) and 407 (NT 26/37), grid reference NT 221707

miles 0	1	2	3	4	5	6	7	8	9	10 miles
kms 0	1 2 3 4 5	6 7 8	9 10 11 12	13 14 15 kms						

◔ 2 hours

▭ On mostly excellent paths by canal, river and disused railway line

P At start of walk at the Tickled Trout Inn or in nearby side streets

T Numerous buses from the centre of Edinburgh

🍴 The Tickled Trout Inn at start of walk and the Royal Scot Inn in Colinton village — both have bar food.

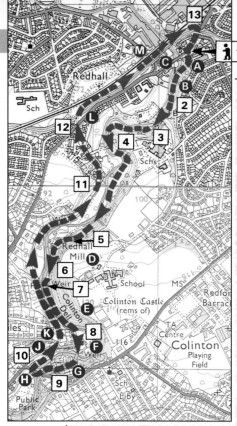

COLINTON

The walk begins at the Tickled Trout Inn on Lanark Road.

1 Take the dirt track that leaves the roadside left of the inn and curves behind it. Beside the Water of Leith **A** it becomes a woodland path through Craiglockhart Dell **B**. Immediately beyond the inn, the broken-down Slateford weir **C** can be viewed by a short detour to the riverbank.

2 Soon a pipeline that bridges the river is reached and immediately afterwards the path forks. Keep right on the riverside path and follow it across a small stream (bridge) beside which is an old dome-shaped stone shelter. On the far side of the stream the path rises and falls to negotiate some riverside rocks then passes a footbridge over the Water of Leith. Pause to view the river from the bridge but do not cross; keep to the near side.

3 At another fork, keep right down some wooden steps to follow the main path across a riverside meadow.

4 At a single-arched stone bridge, where there are some picnic tables, do not cross the river but keep straight on. The well-constructed path continues its meandering way along the near riverbank amongst trees and across meadows.

5 The path joins a dirt track at yet another bridge over the Water of Leith. Again do not cross the river, but keep straight on between some houses to reach the end of a tarmac road. The building at the water's edge here is Redhall Mill **D**.

6 Turn right at the road to follow a dirt track that soon becomes a path. The path descends steps, crosses the lade (mill-stream) that formerly fed Redhall Mill and turns left to form a fine route between the lade and the river.

THE WALK

7 Soon you reach the weir that feeds the lade. You finally cross the river at a wooden bridge in the heart of Colinton Dell **E**. On the far side of the bridge keep left and, avoiding all paths that branch to the right, stay beside the river until the path leads you to the foot of a flight of steps. Climb the steps to emerge onto a tarmac road beside the grounds of Colinton parish church.

8 Keep to the road as it joins Spylaw Bank Road and passes the iron gates at the church **F** entrance. Once past the church, the road bears right, crosses a bridge over the Water of Leith and climbs into Colinton village **G** at Spylaw Street. The Royal Scot Inn is on the right near the top.

9 A few paces beyond the inn, iron gates on the right mark the entrance to Spylaw Park and a sign reads 'Spylaw House'. Take the dirt track that descends from here to the Water of Leith, passing under a high, multi-arched road bridge, then crossing the river at a concrete bridge to enter Spylaw Park. Spylaw House **H** stands beside the river. There is a children's playground in the far corner of the park.

10 On the far side of the bridge, turn right in front of a small stone building then climb the steps beside it to reach the disused railway line **J** above. Turn right under the arch of the bridge to follow the line of the old railway through Easter Hailes Gate tunnel **K** and along a level route high above the Water of Leith back towards the starting point of the walk.

11 At a fork about ½ mile (800 metres) beyond the tunnel keep left, then continue to keep left as the line veers away from the Water of Leith to pass under a small bridge and reach Lanark Road.

12 Two consecutive bridges carry the line across Lanark Road and the Union Canal **L**. Once over the canal bridge, turn right down some steps to join the canal towpath then left along it. The canal soon crosses Slateford aqueduct **M** and bears right to cross Slateford Road.

13 On the nearside of the Slateford bridge, a flight of wooden steps leads down to the roadside. Descend the steps and turn right at the bottom. The Tickled Trout Inn lies a few hundred paces up the road, which can be crossed at traffic lights beneath the canal bridge.

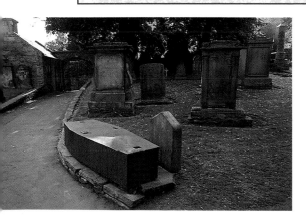

◀ *This mortsafe was hired out to prevent 'body-snatchers' from exhuming cadavers to sell to anatomy classes.*

variety of buildings spanning the past four centuries. The parish church **F**, rebuilt in 1909, stands on the site of a church dating back at least to the 11th century.

Further on is the point where an off-shoot of the Edinburgh-Glasgow railway reached Colinton in 1874. The line **J** was closed in 1967 and now forms a fine walking route through Colinton Dell. The eerie Easter Hailes Gate tunnel **K** is a long, curving and dimly-lit structure, with an uneven surface and a constantly dripping roof.

Soon after, you come to the Union Canal **L**. The Colinton area has one of its finest stretches, with a 600-foot (183-metre), eight-arched aqueduct **M** that gives fine views over the city.

GLYN SATTERLEY

ARTHUR'S SEAT

26

◄ *Salisbury Craigs, backed by the brooding bulk of Arthur's Seat. Few capitals have such dramatic scenery in the city limits. Greylag geese (below left) occur on St Margaret's Loch.*

FACT FILE

❋ Holyrood, on the eastern edge of Edinburgh

▭ Pathfinder 407 (NT 27/37), grid reference NT 270737

miles 0 1 2 3 4 5 6 7 8 9 10 miles
kms 0 1 2 3 4 5 6 7 8 9 10 11 12 13 14 15 kms

◐ Allow 3 hours

▬ Good paths with 700 feet (200m) of ascent. Wear trainers

P Free car park at start

T Edinburgh is well served by trains and coaches and has frequent local buses

🍴 Numerous pubs, restaurants and cafés in Edinburgh

WC Near car park

⌷ Palace of Holyroodhouse is open all year except during royal visits; admission charge

I Tourist information at palace and Waverley Station

An ascent of the hill that dominates Edinburgh's skyline

Arthur's Seat is one of the great landmarks of Edinburgh. At 822 feet (251m), its summit affords an unrivalled view of Scotland's capital and its surroundings, from the Pentland Hills in the south to the Firth of Forth and beyond in the north. Few cities have such rugged hills within their boundaries, and a bracing walk up Arthur's Seat on a fine day is a superb way of escaping from the noise and bustle of the city.

MURDER AT THE PALACE

The walk starts outside the Palace of Holyroodhouse **Ⓐ**, which stands impressively at the eastern end of the Royal Mile. The palace has been the scene of many turbulent events. Mary Queen of Scots lived here for six years and, in 1558, witnessed the murder of her great favourite, the Italian secretary Rizzio, in the

audience chamber. Serious fires destroyed much of the buildings in both 1543 and 1650. Many Scottish kings were married in the palace and Bonnie Prince Charlie held court here, albeit briefly, in 1745.

The name 'Holyrood' is said to originate from a 'holy rood' or cross, which saved the life of King David I in an encounter with a stag near Salisbury Craigs. The king took the 'holy rood' back to Edinburgh

▶ *The Palace of Holyroodhouse and, behind it, the flanks of Whinny Hill rising upwards in Holyrood Park.*

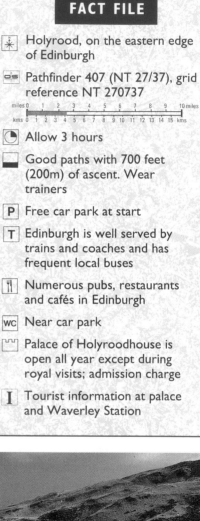

THE WALK

HOLYROOD PARK

The walk begins at the car park belonging to the Palace of Holyroodhouse Ⓐ.

1 Cross the road from the car park and take the obvious path which climbs steeply to the right below Salisbury Craigs Ⓑ. Follow this up and around the west side of the hill. The gradient levels off and then you descend slightly.

2 Just before the path joins the road, take a path to the left through the gap between Cat Nick and Arthur's Seat. Ⓒ. Wooden steps ascend to the north of the summit, to a level, grassy shoulder. Continue along the path around the north-eastern shoulder of the hill, then follow an obvious rocky path that leads to the summit.

3 Retrace the route to the grassy shoulder between Arthur's Seat and Whinny Hill. From here, a conspicuous path leads down an obvious valley west of Whinny Hill, bounded on the left by crags. Follow this path down the hill, bearing left at the bottom to join a good metalled footpath that leads you back to the main road and the car park where the walk began.

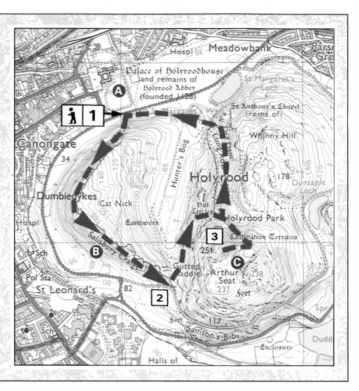

Castle, where he was later commanded, in a dream, to found an abbey. This he did in 1128.

Holyrood Abbey was partly demolished during the Reformation and fell into its current ruined state in the 18th century. It became overshadowed by the palace, which originated as a guesthouse for the Scottish monarchy. Successive generations of monarchs added to the palace and today it is the Queen's official residence in Scotland.

ANNUAL TATTOO

From here, a steep path ascends the western slopes of Cat Nick, with good views over the palace. The path is flanked by Salisbury Craigs Ⓑ on the left, and steep slopes dropping away to the right. As the path gains height, the views over Edinburgh open up. Edinburgh Castle is clearly visible, dominating the city centre. This most famous of Scottish castles dates from Norman times. The Military Tattoo is held here during the annual Edinburgh Festival in August.

Holyrood Park, the annual venue for Fringe Sunday, when actors, fire-eaters and countless other entertainers showcase their talents in a carnival atmosphere, is a wonderful green lung on the edge of the city. Its five crags and peaks, three lochs and grassy, flowered acres are where local people come to relax.

Arthur's Seat Ⓒ is an ancient, weatherbeaten volcano. From its peak there are fine views in all directions. A view dial points out the features beyond the city boundaries. To the north are Leith Docks and the Firth of Forth, with Fife along the northern horizon. The Pentlands lie to the south and the coast is clearly visible stretching away to the east. To the west is the city, with the Old Town dominated by the castle and St Giles' Cathedral—Edinburgh's High Kirk.

CROWDED CAPITAL

Edinburgh began as a small settlement on the ridge leading up to the castle, and grew slowly, only being recognized as the capital of Scotland at the end of the 15th century. By the 18th century it had become very overcrowded, with 20 times more people living in the Old Town than there are today.

The North Bridge was completed in 1772 and a New Town was created north of present-day Princes Street. By the 19th century, the Old Town had become exceedingly run-down, with some of the worst slums in the country. Recent restoration schemes are recreating some of the best of its old character.

From the summit of Arthur's Seat the route leads down a valley below Whinny Hill towards St Margaret's Loch. From here it is a short distance back to the car park.

◀ *The view north from Arthur's Seat encompasses the palace, Leith Docks, the Firth of Forth and the Fife coast.*

SIMON FRASER

◄*The view across Linlithgow Loch to the ruined Linlithgow Palace and St Michael's Church. The reed bunting (inset) may be seen perched on vegetation at the side of the loch.*

with a Gothic fountain, a wedding gift from James V to his queen, Mary of Guise. On 8 December 1542, Mary gave birth to a daughter at the palace. Six days later, her husband died and the tiny Mary Stuart became Queen of Scotland.

HISTORIC CHURCH

Adjoining the palace is St Michael's Church **C**, where Mary was baptized. A handsome building, now carefully restored, it predates the palace and has its own colourful history. In 1645, when the plague raged in the capital, the University of Edinburgh held its classes here. Five years later, following the Battle of Dunbar, Cromwell's troops took possession of both the palace and the church; the roundhead soldiers were billeted in the triforium, their horses stabled in the nave. St Michael's anachronistic aluminium spire adds a somewhat incongruous touch to the skyline. Created in 1964 by the sculptor Geoffrey Clarke, it

A stroll around a historic royal town and its lovely natural loch

The royal town of Linlithgow has associations with many of the Stuart monarchs, but it is the romantic and tragic Mary Queen of Scots, who could have been mistress of three thrones but lost the one she had, who dominates this walk.

You begin in the Kirkgate **A**, one of the most ancient parts of the town. Its origins lie in the 12th century, when David I of Scotland established a manor house here, overlooking the loch. A tight cluster of medieval huts grew up, sheltering beneath its protective shadow.

Linlithgow Palace **B**, on the site of David's manor, dominates the surrounding countryside. An impressive ruin, ravaged by time and fire, it still exudes an air of dignified splendour — an appropriate birthplace for a queen. Few medieval Scottish buildings are on such a grand scale. Begun in 1425 for James I, it was completed over a century later by James IV and V.

Its halls and chambers, now roofless, surround a central quadrangle

FACT FILE

* Linlithgow, 18 miles (28.8km) west of Edinburgh

* Pathfinders 405 (NS 87/97) and 406 (NT 07/17), grid reference NT 001771

miles 0 1 2 3 4 5 6 7 8 9 10 miles
kms 0 1 2 3 4 5 6 7 8 9 10 11 12 13 14 15 kms

* Allow 1 hour

* Town roads and lochside paths

* **P** Free car park in Market Lane at the start

* **T** BR mainline service

* Cafés, restaurants, pubs and hotels in Linlithgow

* **WC** In the car park at the start

* **I** Information Centre in the Town House, near the start

THE WALK

LINLITHGOW

The walk begins in the car park south-west of Linlithgow Palace, near the Information Centre.

1 Turn left out of the car park towards The Cross, then turn left again to walk along Kirkgate **A** to the palace **B**.

2 Retrace your steps past St Michael's Church **C** downhill to The Cross. Bear left and pass between the Town House (Information Centre) and The Cross Well **D**.

3 Turn left into High Street. At a traffic island, bear left down Blackness Road. After about ¼ mile (400m), at the end of the residential area, turn left through a kissing-gate onto a dirt path across a field, to Linlithgow Loch **E**.

4 Bear right and follow the path to the next kissing-gate. Bear left around the contours of the loch to a gated entrance before the Palace. Turn right, and climb the steps beside a stone wall to return to the car park.

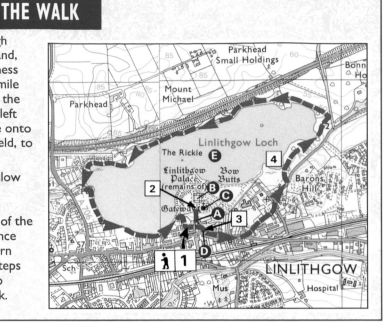

▲*From Linlithgow Palace there are fine views of the countryside to the north and of the surrounding town.*

represents a crown of thorns piercing the heavens, a strikingly modern design in an almost timeless setting.

On a wall opposite Cross House is a stone carving marking the entrance to the Debtor's Prison. This was the site of the old fire-pump, an appliance dragged to emergencies by horses stabled nearby. The horses had a dual role as they also pulled the town hearse. Unfortunately, they often operated in a state of confusion, sedately pacing to an inferno or galloping full pelt at the head of a funeral cortege!

ELABORATE FOUNTAIN

In the centre of the square stands The Cross Well **D**, a beautifully carved fountain that marks the site of the old market cross. This elaborately adorned hexagonal well, with its delicately carved figures surmounted by a unicorn, is a true

BOTH PHOTOS: JASON SMALLEY

work of art. It is even more remarkable when one thinks it was built literally single-handed in 1806; its creator, mason Robert Gray, had only one hand, in which he held his chisel, while a mallet was strapped to the stump of his other arm. The square was the venue for public executions until about 130 years ago.

The route continues around the edges of Linlithgow Loch **E**, one of only two natural lochs in the Lothians. These waters once played an important role in the leather trade. Cromwell's troops instructed the locals in the art of tanning, and by the 18th century there were 17 tanneries in Linlithgow. Raw hides were soaked in a solution of loch water and oak bark to provide the necessary tannin.

Mute swans have nested on the banks of the loch for centuries, though it is claimed that they left when Cromwell's army entered the town, and returned only when Charles II was restored to the throne. The swans are very much in evidence today, the cob's relatively large bill knob distinguishing him from the female, who carries and broods her cygnets on her back, beneath enfolding wings.

Linlithgow Loch provides an ideal habitat for reed buntings, sedge warblers, common sandpipers, coots, moorhens and a wide variety of very tame and extremely vocal ducks. Great crested grebes provide the most fascinating spring

spectacle, performing their quaint courtship display, which includes head shaking and the presentation of waterweeds; posturing high out of the water, their feet patter noisily on the surface of the loch.

THE END OF AN ERA

From every viewpoint, the lovely ruin of the palace dominates the scene, evoking memories of one of the most controversial characters of Scottish history. Eventually exiled by her subjects, a victim of the ever changing fortunes of Scottish history, Mary Stuart left behind many enigmas. Her reign was the end of an era for Scotland — the end of independence — yet her memory lingers, in art and literature, but most of all in Linlithgow, where she was born and began her brief reign.

▼*Though the palace's halls have lost their roofs it is easy to see how impressive the buildings once were.*

A hike across the grouse moors of the Lammermuir Hills

The wild, windswept and lonely Lammermuir Hills provided the inspiration for both Sir Walter Scott's romantic novel *The Bride of the Lammermoors* and Donizetti's opera *Lucia di Lammermoor*.

In earlier times, the hills formed part of the estates of the abbeys of Kelso and Melrose, and were used not only to graze sheep and cattle, but also to isolate wayward members of those religious communities in a state of penitential solitary confinement. Today, the vast tracts of hillside foster sheep and red grouse.

Stoneypath **A**, near the start of the walk, is a typical small hill farm, grazing around 1,500 black-faced sheep. The red sandstone farm building is dated 1720. Associated with it, on the Jinkie Burn, is a water

▲*As you climb a broad track up Clints Law, the view behind you includes the pyramidal North Berwick Law on the horizon. Look out for the adder (female shown left), which enjoys these moors.*

FACT FILE

✳ Stoneypath, 5 miles (8km) south-west of Dunbar, off the B6370

🗺 Pathfinders 409 (NT 67/77) and 422 (NT 66/76), grid reference NT 614712

miles 0 1 2 3 4 5 6 7 8 9 10 miles
kms 0 1 2 3 4 5 6 7 8 9 10 11 12 13 14 15 kms

◔ Allow 5 hours

▲ A long, sometimes strenuous walk with a few steep ascents and descents. The wild, marshy moors can be muddy, and are occasionally used for grouse-shooting in season (12 Aug-10 Dec). Weatherproof clothing and good boots are essential. Take food and a compass

🅿 Space at the start

🍴 None on the route; nearest is the Garvald Hotel in Garvald, 1½ miles (2.4km) south-west of the start

mill which once powered a straw-buncher and bruiser.

A track leaves the farmyard and swings up through gorse and fox-gloves towards Moorcock Hall **B**, a sturdy stone house that, until recently, was occupied by a hill shepherd.

As you skirt a turnip field on the way up to Clints Law, the track becomes heavily rutted. Here, there is a fine view **C** behind you of East Lothian and, across the Firth of Forth, the outline of Fife. To your left, as you face north-west, is the humpbacked silhouette of Traprain Law, where an important hoard of

▼*The walk begins on the road next to Stoneypath cottages, where there is space for parking your car.*

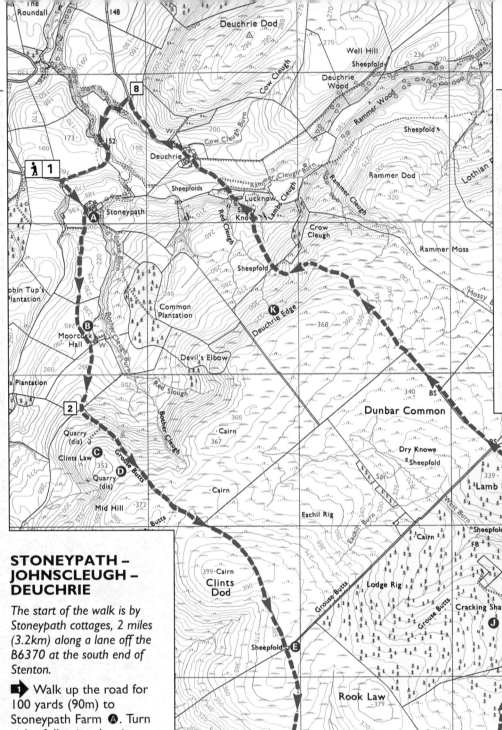
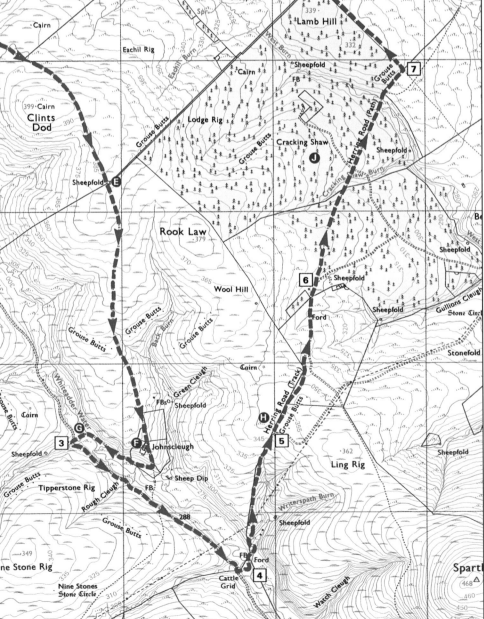

down to a gate at a sheepfold **E** by a wooden hut. Beyond the gate, continue straight ahead on the track, dropping gently to Johnscleugh Farm **F**. Go through two farm gates and take the metalled farm road, which doubles back across the Whiteadder Water **G** to a road.

3 Turn left and continue over the ford across Rough Cleugh. The road winds past a red wooden railway carriage. Shortly beyond the line of pylons, bear left to a ford over the

STONEYPATH – JOHNSCLEUGH – DEUCHRIE

The start of the walk is by Stoneypath cottages, 2 miles (3.2km) along a lane off the B6370 at the south end of Stenton.

1 Walk up the road for 100 yards (90m) to Stoneypath Farm **A**. Turn right, following the sign for Johnscleugh, on a rough farm track climbing between mildly electrified cattle-fences. Continue ahead past Moorcock Hall **B**. Keeping the wire fence to your left, follow the rutted track, with good views **C** behind you, towards Clints Law. Go through the gate halfway up the hill.

2 Take the stony track and climb steeply past the summit of Clints Law and the grouse butts **D**. Beyond Clints Dod on your right, you go gently

Whiteadder Water.

▶4 Cross the ford and join the Herring Road Ⓗ (marked with black-and-white posts), which climbs steeply up from the valley floor. You recross the line of pylons. At the top of the hill, the track veers right.

▶5 Carry on straight ahead along the line of the fence, through a gate. Eventually, you join a wide road. Turn left, to a corrugated-iron hut at the far corner of a small wood.

▶6 Turn left off the road, past the hut and over the grass, making diagonally for the barbed wire fence of the plantation Ⓙ. A public footpath sign points towards you over the barbed wire. Cross the wire with care. Follow the right-of-way down a broad swathe through the conifers. Continue on the same heading, though the track itself is not always clearly visible. Take care crossing the marshy area around Cracking Shaw Burn. Soon after, you reach the road that bisects the plantation. Look for another public footpath sign, leading on in the same direction. Go straight on across the West Burn, where the ground becomes marshy again. Jump the narrow (but deep) burn, and go up the very steep grassy bank opposite, making for the grouse butts ahead on the hilltop. Follow the fence to the corner of the plantation.

▶7 Turn left. Follow the fences to a junction of four fences. Follow the fence ahead over Dunbar Common. Where it turns left, keep on in the same direction to Deuchrie Edge Ⓚ. Follow the track downhill, bending left, then right and through a sheepfold. Continue down to the stone farmhouse at Lucknow. Go through the gate and continue downhill, to the farm buildings at Deuchrie. Continue through the farm and down past the two sets of houses to a junction.

▶8 Turn left and follow the metalled road, over the ford, back to Stoneypath.

▲ *The route leads down to Lucknow. The way across the moors is punctuated by grouse butts (below), hiding places for the 'guns' who wait for the birds to be driven over.*

Roman silver was discovered earlier this century. Ahead is the pyramidal North Berwick Law, where witches were once burnt and, in the Firth, the Bass Rock, formerly a prison but now a sanctuary for seabirds.

TRACKING FOOTFALLS

The arm of a solar-powered seismographic transmitter on the hillside to your right is part of the work of the Global Seismology Research Group based at the British Geological Survey in Edinburgh. It records motion and movement — it is sensitive even to a walker's footsteps — with a view to establishing the risk of earthquakes in the area.

The path runs between stands of

▲ *Across the valley of Whiteadder Water stands Johnscleugh Farm.*

pink bell heather and bracken and passes the first of many grouse butts Ⓓ, wooden frames thickly woven with heather. In use only two or three days a year, between times they offer the walker shelter from wind, snow or rain.

Patches of marshy ground appear beside the path as you pass the summits of Mid Hill and Clints Dod. Skylarks and meadow pipits flit unexpectedly out of the heather, and seagulls wheel overhead when driven inland by bad weather. Far off to your right is Edinburgh, with the outline of Arthur's Seat and the Pentland Hills clearly visible.

ALL PHOTOS: MICHAEL TURNBULL

A wide plain bordered by hills opens in front as you reach a simple wooden sheepfold **E**, an old hut and trailer used to store fodder for the sheep. Ahead, an occasional flash of reflected sunlight reveals the distant surface of the 1½-mile-long (2.4-km) Whiteadder Reservoir.

◄ *This footbridge hints at the scene when the river, here a mere trickle, floods. Heather is burnt (below) to encourage the new growth on which grouse prefer to feed.*

WELCOME WATER

You descend gently to Johnscleugh farm **F**, which stands on the site of an old pele tower. Its position on a spur above the Whiteadder Valley commands the road south. The chief shepherd of King Loth of Lothian supposedly lived here.

You walk through the farmyard in the shade of ancient trees. There are views of Whiteadder Water **G**, a welcome sight after the desolation of the hills, even though it is a mere trickle in a broad alluvial plain.

The route crosses the river and continues along a road on the far side of the valley. The hum of electricity pylons can be heard as you walk down again to the wide ford, where you recross the river.

Before the ford is a cattle grid and beside it is a white wooden footbridge, necessary on those days when the river is in spate and torrents of water pour down this valley. The route turns north along the ancient Herring Road **H** (see box) and follows a line of pylons back into the hills. The stone chips of the road give way to a deeply rutted track through the heather. This becomes a broad forestry road that runs past a small wood on your left.

At the road's far end stands a corrugated iron hut. Here, the route — still following the line of the Herring Road — crosses the grass to reach the edge of the large Cracking Shaw plantation **J**. A broad swathe of grass and heather takes you through the young evergreen trees and over the Cracking Shaw Burn.

You cross another road and then go over the broader Wet Burn, where shoals of minnows can be seen darting among the weeds in the clear, refreshing waters.

FINAL VIEWS

The route clambers above the stream up the steep slopes of Lamb Hill. At the top, there are views to your right down into the valley of the Mossy Burn. You turn north-west along the edge of the plantation. Once you are past the trees, you can see Dry Knowe sheepfold to your left, standing beside a ruined, stone shepherd's cottage.

Along this section of the walk, adders can be seen basking in the sun. Their natural tendency is to avoid walkers unless they are provoked, but be wary about where you are putting your feet. This is especially true in cold weather, when they are sluggish.

The walk down the steep side of Deuchrie Edge **K** gives you more magnificent views of the Firth of Forth, and you may see a pheasant's bright colours, or a dark lizard in the grass. Beyond the pink-roofed farm buildings at Deuchrie, you follow a road back to Stoneypath.

The Herring Road

The Herring Road was never a road as such, rather a disjointed series of tracks that formed a route between Dunbar and Lauder. Today, it can be traced easily only in a few sections.

This ancient route owes its name, and its existence, to the huge catches of herring landed at the port of Dunbar between the 17th and 19th centuries. In the industry's heyday, 20,000 men and women came to the town in late summer every year to process the catches from nearly 300 boats, which cast their nets among the great herring shoals of the North Sea.

Once the herring had been gutted and salted by the fishwives of Dunbar, they were packed into barrels and transported by packhorse or cart along the Herring Road to Lauder. Farmers from the Tweed Valley would come up the road to Dunbar at Lammastide to stock up with fish for the winter.

The Herring Road was not used only by those engaged in the fish trade. Drovers used it to take sheep and cattle to the fairs, while smugglers and wreckers saw it as a convenient route for escaping the law. Today, its remaining sections make a fine path for walkers exploring the Lammermuir Hills.

These 19th-century fishwives found seasonal employment gutting and packing the huge catches of North Sea herring at Dunbar.

◀ *The grassy hillsides of the Ochils are complemented by spectacular woodland scenery. (above) Dollar Academy, a private school, in its grounds.*

An energetic walk to the romantic Castle Campbell

The walk begins in the small town of Dollar on the northern edge of the lowlands and leads up the glen to the impressive Castle Campbell. Partially ruined, stern, romantic and in an unrivalled setting, it is everything a castle should be, and is surrounded by tales and legends, embracing a *Who's Who* of history. John Knox preached there, Mary Queen of Scots visited it, Montrose's men sacked it and Cromwell's General Monck burnt it.

BURNSIDE PATHS

The castle's name was originally Gloume, with its guardian burns of Care and Sorrow. An act of parliament allowed the new Campbell owners to change the name of their castle, but the burn names survive and they unite below the castle rock to become the Dollar Burn. The town's name has no monetary origins; an early version was Dolour (pain), in keeping, perhaps, with the nearby Castle Gloume!

The walk follows Dollar Burn up to the copybook castle, and the Ochil scarp ensures it is uphill all the way. Cherry trees line the early walk upstream and the old church can be seen above the Middle Bridge, built so the first rector of the famous Dollar Academy could cross from manse to school Ⓐ. The school is a neo-classical building

Waterfalls tumble down the glens which criss-cross the Ochils landscape.

built in 1820 with the money bequeathed by a local shepherd boy, John McNabb, who ran away to sea and became a rich sea captain.

The steep-sided glen Ⓑ has a certain grandeur and is most impressive after rain when the gorges echo wildly with torrents of water. Woodcocks love the rich tree cover and the waters are the habitat of the bold dippers. Wooden walkways and bridges are built within the gorge itself, the sides of which rise up to almost 180 feet (56 metres). The 15th-century castle Ⓒ is built above it, although this cannot be

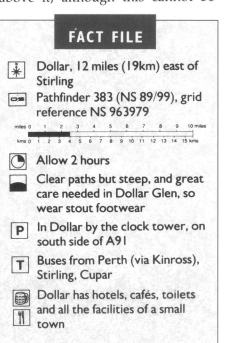

FACT FILE

- ✴ Dollar, 12 miles (19km) east of Stirling
- ▭ Pathfinder 383 (NS 89/99), grid reference NS 963979

miles 0   1   2   3   4   5   6   7   8   9   10 miles
kms 0   1 2 3   4   5 6 7   8 9 10 11 12 13 14 15 kms

- ◔ Allow 2 hours
- ⌒ Clear paths but steep, and great care needed in Dollar Glen, so wear stout footwear
- Ⓟ In Dollar by the clock tower, on south side of A91
- Ⓣ Buses from Perth (via Kinross), Stirling, Cupar
- 🏨🍴 Dollar has hotels, cafés, toilets and all the facilities of a small town

THE WALK

DOLLAR–CASTLE CAMPBELL

The walk begins at the clock tower in Dollar just south of the A91 on the west bank of the burn.

1 Walk up the west bank of the burn (West Burnside) from the A91, passing an old bridge and a fountain. Just beyond these, turn left along Academy Place to reach the school grounds of Dollar Academy **A** . Return to the Burnside.

2 At the head of the West Burnside cross the narrow bridge (no pavement). Turn immediately left by a notice board on to a footpath up the east bank to reach the area known as the Mill Green.

3 Take the steep path at the far end of the Mill Green, then follow the well-kept wooden walkway (steps and hand rails). Turn left at the hair-pin bend and walk into the gorge **B** ,

following the walkways and crossing the bridges. The going is steep, rough and exposed, and it can be dangerous here, so keep children well away from the edge, and keep dogs on leads. Turn left at the next fork and continue uphill out of the gorge until reaching the castle **C** on the right. Paths further up the burn lead to several pretty waterfalls **D** .

4 Leave the castle by turning right at the bottom of its drive. Follow the sign reading 'Public Footpath — Glendevon' by the solitary cottage **E** , and walk for a few yards to see the view of the castle and beyond. Continue on the small, narrow road past a lay-by. Cross the cattle grid and pass Gloom Hill quarry **F** car park on the left. Walk down the steep road to the Dollar Burn. Continue along the East Burnside to the clock tower.

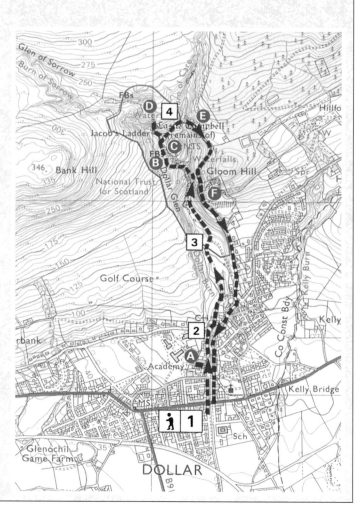

◄ *Built by the first Earl of Argyll, Castle Campbell stands majestically above Dollar. Gloom Hill quarry (inset) is popular with climbers.*

seen from the gorge. All along the burn there is a succession of pretty waterfalls and quiet corners and beyond the route there is an exceptionally tranquil spot **D** where they can be viewed at leisure.

AND DOWN AGAIN

From the castle entrance, with its hanging tree, a tiny road leads past a white cottage **E** which has a commanding view of the Lowlands and the hill of White Wisp behind. Many consider this to be the best view of the castle. As the road descends, the secretive quarry of Gloom Hill **F** lies to the left, its abandoned walls making good sport for rock climbers. The road drops steadily downhill to the old town and so back to the Burnside and the start of the walk.

THE HILL OF THE FAIRIES

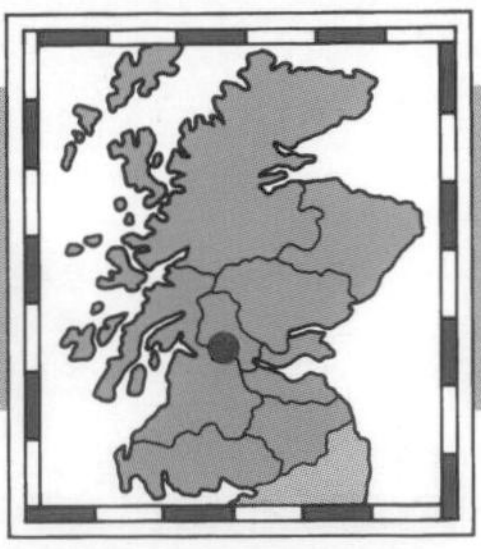

JOHN WATNEY

A hill walk in the heart of the Trossachs

This pleasant hill walk follows a route from the village of Strathyre Ⓐ, a place made famous through the Scots music hall song, *Bonnie Strathyre*. Beinn an t-Sidhein Ⓑ, pronounced Ben an Shee-an, which overlooks the area, is 'the hill of the fairy people'. Many hills like this one in Scotland are associated with the fairy folk, but these fairies should not be confused with the delicate little fairies of childhood. The highland fairy folk were sometimes kind, but more often cruel and mischievous. A church minister from nearby Balquhidder, the Reverend Robert Kirk, was an expert in the lore and published a book in the 17th century called *The Secret Commonwealth of Elves, Fauns and Fairies*. It is claimed that his body was eventually spirited away to the fairy kingdom.

The view from the summit of the hill is extensive, with lochs and mountains dominating the scene. Looking straight ahead, Loch Lubnaig stretches away to the south, and on the marshes close to where the River Balvag enters the loch is the site of an ancient crannog, a building which floated like an island home.

BIRDS AND ANIMALS

While forestry has often been accused of stifling wildlife, the buffer zones between the heavily planted trees and the open hillside, such as at the top of Beinn an t-Sidhein, are well populated by both birds and animals. Along the forest paths the belling of tits and the sharp song of chaffinch can be heard. Closer to the edge of the trees there are many more birds to be seen and heard, especially great tits and blue tits, willow warblers, chiff-chaffs and blackbirds. Out on the open hillside buzzards may be seen, along with skylarks and meadow pipits, curlews and lapwing and, lower down, oystercatchers. Roe deer sometimes

FACT FILE

- Strathyre, on the A84
- Pathfinder 358 (NN 41/51), grid reference NN 560172

miles 0 1 2 3 4 5 6 7 8 9 10 miles
kms 0 1 2 3 4 5 6 7 8 9 10 11 12 13 14 15 kms

- Allow 3 hours
- Steep at first, then levelling out. Good forestry tracks and hill paths. Good waterproof boots recommended
- Public car park in Strathyre
- Public toilets in Strathyre. Also shops, café, hotels

▲ ***Beinn an t-Sidhein, scene of folklore. (below) Rob Roy, Highland outlaw, is buried in nearby Balquhidder.***

MARY EVANS PICTURE LIBRARY

THE WALK

STRATHYRE – BEINN AN T-SIDHEIN

The walk begins at the old bridge over the River Balvag, next to the car park in Strathyre village ⒶⒶ on the A84.

1 Walk down Strathyre main street to a crossroads where the Munro Hotel stands. Take the road down to the left, leading away from the hotel. It is also signposted as a cycle path to Callander. Cross the old bridge, pass the St John's Holiday Home for the Blind on the left and come to a road junction.

2 Walk a few yards along the road until reaching a signposted track on the opposite side which leads uphill. The blue markers indicate Beinn an t-Sidhein.

3 At a forestry road, turn right and continue to another sign and a pole with blue, green and yellow markings. Follow its direction uphill.

4 Another forest road is soon reached where there are two markers. Follow the blue marker, left, still climbing uphill. Keep to a well-walked forest path and do not take any paths branching off to the right unless signposted by a blue marker. Once clear of the forest and on the open hillside follow a clear hill path until it branches into two. Take the path to the right going uphill until reaching the summit of Beinn an t-Sidhein Ⓑ.

5 From the summit, either descend the same way or continue over the hill on a faint hill path for about 2 miles (3.2 km) over Buachaille Breige Ⓒ, a little rocky outcrop, towards an obvious break in the forest on the right. Just beyond the break, a forestry road goes down through the forest to Stroneslaney Ⓓ on the old Strathyre to Balquhidder road. Turn left to visit Balquhidder which is 4 miles (6.4 km) away, or turn right and follow the road back through the forest to Strathyre.

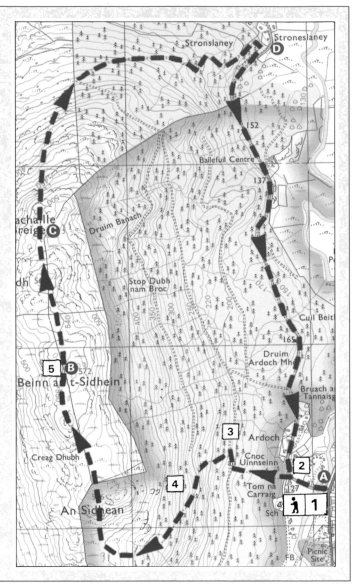

JOHN WATNEY

◄ *Strathyre, set in a beautiful forest, is ringed by steep hills. It is a centre for hillwalkers and anglers.*

▼ *The tree-pipit nests in the forest.*

A P BARNES NHPA

browse on these slopes in the early morning and evenings and the red fox creeps his silent way to and from the glen below, but he is not a common sight, especially in daylight.

Below, in Glen Buckie, there is an atmosphere of highland remoteness. History abounds hereabouts. Sir Walter Scott set his *Lady of the Lake* in this area and describes the clansmen rousing the clan to battle by carrying the Fiery Cross around the district. The cross was carried along 'Balvag's swampy course'.

Many people return to Strathyre at this point but it is well worthwhile descending the long northern shoulder of Beinn an t-Sidhein by Buachaille Breige Ⓒ to the forest track that climbs the hill from Stroneslaney Ⓓ. This was the site of a 13th-century battle which took place between the MacLarens and Buchanans. Not far from here, and well worth a short detour from this walk, is the village of Balquhidder, which is the final resting place of Rob Roy, a one-time chief of the Clan MacGregor who was made immortal by the pen of Sir Walter Scott. His grave can be seen in the village churchyard.

TO THE WHANGIE

CENTRAL

From the Queen's View to the Whangie rock face

The focus of this walk, which is north-east of Glasgow, is a 300-foot (90-metre) long rock face, some 50 feet (15 metres) in height. This rugged face, known as the Whangie, has been cleft in two all the way along its length. There are two explanations for this, one legendary and one factual.

DEVIL'S WORK

The story goes that the Devil himself created what is a spectacular natural phenomenon. According to this legend, the Devil had been holding a meeting with local warlocks on the nearby Campsie Fells. As he flew over the area en route to another

FACT FILE

- On the edge of Stockie Muir, by A809 Bearsden to Drymen road.

- Pathfinder 403 (NS 47/57) and 391 (NS 48/58), grid reference NS 510808

  miles 0 | 1 2 3 4 | 5 6 7 8 9 | 10 miles
  kms 0 | 1 2 3 4 5 6 7 | 8 9 10 11 12 13 14 15 | kms

- Allow 3 hours

- A straightforward hill walk. Strong shoes or boots recommended

- **P** Queen's View car park at beginning of walk

- Cafés, restaurants and hotels in Blanefields and Drymen

- **WC** Public toilets in Drymen

meeting with the witches of Dumbarton, he flicked his tail and cut through the solid rock face.

The result was a shearing of the rock into what you see today: a long, deep chasm that yawns along the line of separation. The walls, which

▲ *The vista from Queen's View stretches across rolling hills to where the Scottish Highlands begin. The chaffinch (inset), with its distinctive markings, is found in deciduous woodland, scrub and bushes.*

soar to about 50 feet (15 metres) in places, form a jagged crest.

However, the more likely, but certainly less colourful, explanation of the phenomenon is that it was created by retreating ice during the closing stages of the Ice Age. A moving glacier probably caused the volcanic rock to fracture.

HIGHLAND VIEW

The Queen's View **A**, at the start of the walk, is on the A809 Bearsden to Drymen road. It is a popular stopping place for locals and visitors alike, for here, on the edge of the Stockie Muir, there is a view over the fields, woods and rolling hills of Lowland Scotland to where the Highland Boundary Fault marks the beginning of the Highlands.

This great geological fault, which runs in a diagonal line from the Isle of Arran to Aberdeen, separates the

AA PICTURE LIBRARY INSET E. A. JANES/NHPA

31

103

THE WALK

THE WHANGIE

The walk begins at the Queen's View Car Park on the A809 Bearsden to Drymen road.

1 Leave the car park **A** and cross the stile over the drystone dyke. Follow the well-trodden path up the hill and when you reach the top of the hill cross a ladder stile.

2 Follow the well-marked path along the side of the hill without losing any height, until you reach the Whangie itself **B**. The Whangie may be recognised as a 'valley' of rocks. Do not be tempted to take any paths that will lead you up over the top of the hill.

3 Walk through the chasm of the Whangie at its southern end and continue southwards on a faint path down through a small valley. Straight in

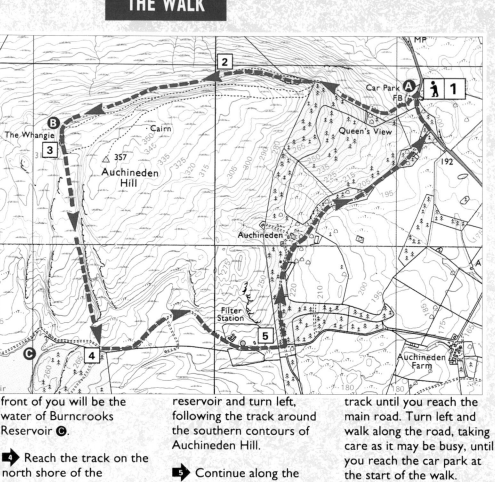

front of you will be the water of Burncrooks Reservoir **C**.

4 Reach the track on the north shore of the

reservoir and turn left, following the track around the southern contours of Auchineden Hill.

5 Continue along the

track until you reach the main road. Turn left and walk along the road, taking care as it may be busy, until you reach the car park at the start of the walk.

◄*The expanse of Burncrooks Reservoir, seen from the crest of Auchineden Hill, adds the element of water to this dramatic landscape of hills and valleys. From the Hill's summit can also be seen the Whangie (right). Legend has it that the cleft splitting this rock face in two is the work of the Devil.*

BOTH PHOTOS TOM WIER

mountains and glens of the Highlands from the gentle Lowlands. And nowhere can it be seen better than from here.

Across the flats of the Muir, Ben Lomond, the most southerly mountain in Scotland, lifts its head from the island-dotted waters of Loch Lomond. But the scenery has more to offer. To the left of the mountain, the Luss hills and the distant Arrochar Alps form a serrated skyline; to the right, the hills of the

Trossachs dominate. This is the most southern of all the areas in Scotland which can truly be called highland in character. The grandeur of the region has provided literary inspiration: Sir Walter Scott waxed lyrical about the Trossachs in *The Lady of the Lake* and *Rob Roy*.

All the way along the hillside that

leads to the Whangie **B**, the eye is drawn northwards and the scene becomes more dramatic the higher the climb. The final section of the route passes Burncrooks Reservoir **C**, leading along country lanes and tracks and finally arriving back at the A809 road and the car park at the beginning of the walk.

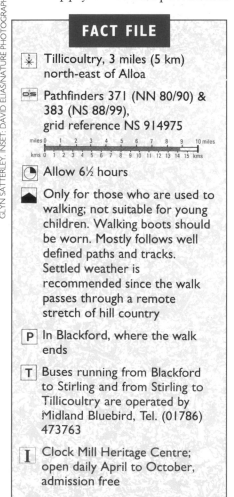

◀ *The Ochils rise majestically from a deep ravine. The bilberry (inset) thrives in mountainous areas and in many places has replaced rival plants such as heather to form 'bilberry moors'.*

from the hills above. The maintained path through the glen crosses over bridges and goes up steps to give high vantage points, which provide fine views of the deep gorge.

POWER SOURCE

Shortly beyond a working quarry, a new bridge is reached, spanning the burn. Below are the remnants of an old wooden dam ❸ — another connection with the weaving industry. Water was an essential power source for the looms, and this dam — an impressive piece of engineering for its day — was built to harness the flowing burn and provide a guaranteed supply of natural power that

GLYN SATTERLEY. INSET: DAVID ELIAS/NATURE PHOTOGRAPHERS LTD

Following in the footsteps of the weavers of old

This is a linear walk along an old trade route through a range of 2,000-foot (610-metre) hills. The walk has a wonderful open aspect, with more of a moorland than a mountain character, and offers some spectacular views. This route would have been used by Tillicoultry weavers 150 years ago as they went to trade their wares with the leather workers of Blackford ❻, 7 miles (11.2 km) away.

The Clock Mill Heritage Centre ❹, at the start of the walk, is a former mill building, built in 1824. It now houses an exhibition of information and machinery relating the history and development of woollen production in the district of Clackmannanshire.

HAND LOOMS

The fascinating exhibition includes traditional hand looms and an audiovisual presentation. A number of craft workers are based upstairs in the building and can be seen working. Alongside the attractive Mill Glen, the tumbling burn rushes down over cascading waterfalls

FACT FILE

❋ Tillicoultry, 3 miles (5 km) north-east of Alloa

🗺 Pathfinders 371 (NN 80/90) & 383 (NS 88/99), grid reference NS 914975

miles 0 1 2 3 4 5 6 7 8 9 10 miles
kms 0 1 2 3 4 5 6 7 8 9 10 11 12 13 14 15 kms

◔ Allow 6½ hours

▲ Only for those who are used to walking; not suitable for young children. Walking boots should be worn. Mostly follows well defined paths and tracks. Settled weather is recommended since the walk passes through a remote stretch of hill country

P In Blackford, where the walk ends

T Buses running from Blackford to Stirling and from Stirling to Tillicoultry are operated by Midland Bluebird, Tel. (01786) 473763

I Clock Mill Heritage Centre; open daily April to October, admission free

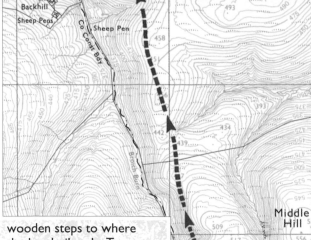

THE WALK

TILLICOULTRY – BLACKFORD

Park your car at the end of the walk in Blackford. Catch a bus to Stirling, then change bus for Tillicoultry (check all bus times in advance), where the walk starts at the Clock Mill information centre. This is reached by walking back towards Stirling from the bus stop in the centre of the village and turning right by the Royal Arms to reach the Clock Mill. NB Because of the bus times from Blackford to Stirling, it is probably inadvisable to attempt this walk without a car.

1 Emerge from the Clock Tower **A** and turn right to go behind it. Turn right again over the bridge crossing the burn and left up a few steps into a paved area with seats and information boards. Ignore the 'Public Footpath to Blackford' sign at the car park. Instead, follow the path straight ahead through the paved area, on the right-hand side of the burn, and pass through a green gate. The path turns left across a bridge and up concrete steps to a rather unsightly working quarry.

2 Continue along the path and up more steps until you reach a new, silver-coloured bridge crossing the burn. Below the new bridge are the remnants of an old dam **B** built to provide a water catchment for the local woollen mills. Cross the silver bridge and go up steps to the right (ignoring a path going straight on) to reach a seat with a good view up the glen to The Law, one of the Ochils' tops. Go along the path to the right to cross another new silver-coloured bridge. Go up concrete, then

wooden steps to where the handrail ends. Turn sharp right here, ignoring the path going down to the left, which leads to the foot of the Law. Follow wooden steps to where the path levels.

3 As soon as the level ground is reached, on a left-hand bend, ignore the path straight on and turn left at right angles onto a rather indistinct track. It leads fairly steeply up the open hillside and in a short distance joins a good, obvious path. Turn left along this and continue, with excellent views of the surrounding hills, and behind you the flat Forth

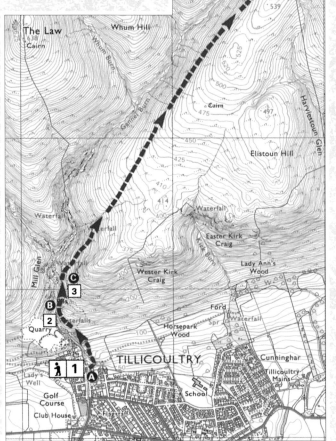

Valley and the River Forth **C**. Proceed gradually uphill with Law Hill always prominent on your left, until you reach a metal fence with a gate in its corner. The path leads on to the left of the fence, bearing away from it, then dips gradually down into the upper reaches of the glen between the hills. The hill now prominent on the left is Andrew Gannel Hill, unnamed on the map but an excellent viewpoint. The path continues very obviously straight on to arrive at a flat, boggy area known as Maddy Moss.

4 The path veers left to avoid the bog and up a short slope. It then bears right and levels to meet a fence under Skythorn Hill. The path now becomes less distinct, but follow the fence on its left, into and out of a dip. Keeping the fence on your right, walk away from it to the left at a shallow angle until you can spot a metal stile in another fence, crossing the first at right angles. Head for the stile and cross it to reach a very prominent, grassy vehicle track — the highest point of the walk.

5 Follow the vehicle track bearing right at first, then left again, with the summit of Skythorn Hill on your right. There are superb views ahead to the high hills **D** of the north, which may well have a covering of snow still visible on them. Also ahead, and below Upper Glendevon Reservoir can be seen from here. The track arrives at a gate, with a stile on its right. Cross the stile and continue on the track straight ahead, making for the right hand end of the reservoir and its

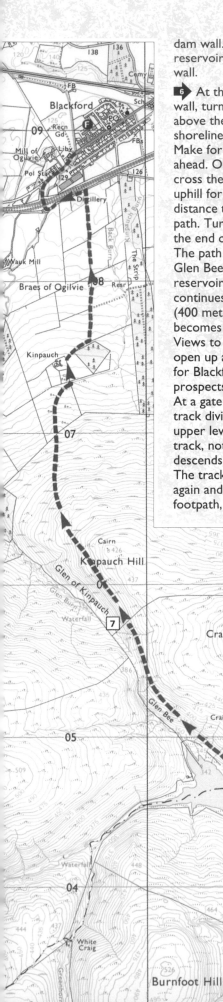

▲*The path hugs the edge of the Ochils, which run the length of a 20-mile- (32-km-) long volcanic fault.*

dam wall. On reaching the reservoir **E**, cross the dam wall.

▶ At the far end of the wall, turn left along a path above the reservoir shoreline, inside a fence. Make for a pine plantation ahead. On reaching this, cross the fence and walk uphill for a very short distance to meet a good path. Turn left along this to the end of the reservoir. The path bears right into Glen Bee. After leaving the reservoir the path continues for ¼ mile (400 metres), then becomes a rough track. Views to the north now open up again as you head for Blackford, with prospects of the high hills. At a gate and stile, the track divides. Take the upper level, right-hand track, not the one that descends steeply to the left. The track becomes grassy again and narrows to a footpath, traversing the

slopes of Kinpauch Hill. The village of Blackford soon comes into view beyond the A9 trunk ahead.

▶ The prominent white building in the village, Tullibardine Distillery, is a good landmark to head for. Descend Kinpauch Hill, keeping well left of the summit, but always heading for Blackford. A grassy path leads down towards some farm buildings. Follow this path until a farm track is reached. Go through a gate and bear right along the stony track, which continues straight on through gates. At the end of the track, at its junction with a minor road, is a prominent, green metal gate with a stile on its left. Cross the stile and turn left along the minor road which leads across the A9 into Blackford **F**. Great care must be taken in negotiating the main road, then walk on into the village.

would last throughout the year.

The path gradually climbs out of the gorge onto the open hillside. Much of the visual attractiveness of the Ochils lies in the dramatic escarpment that plunges down to the towns that have grown up in the valleys. The name 'Ochil' derives from the ancient Celtic word *Uchil*, which means 'high ground'. Millions of years ago, a natural break in the earth's crust occurred near where the town of Stirling now stands and ran east-west for 20 miles (32 km). This is known as the Ochils Fault. It had the effect of 'throwing' down all the land south of it to an original depth of about 10,000 feet (3,000 metres) in the flood plain, which is now silted up.

MADDY MOSS

It is this plain, containing the meandering River Forth **C** and its surrounding farmland and industry, that you look back upon as you pause for breath during your ascent. In summer, the air is filled with the sound of lark song and you may be lucky enough to see a peregrine falcon quartering the ground for prey.

By the time you reach a marshy area known as Maddy Moss, the climbing is largely behind you, and a short time later you are at the watershed and ready to begin your descent to Blackford. To the left is the highest summit of the Ochils, the 2,400-foot (721-metre) Ben Cleuch. The high hills **D** of the north are in evidence here, sometimes partly

ALL PHOTOS GLYN SATTERLEY

▲ *The Upper Glendevon Reservoir is one of two such installations in the glen. The route leads across the dam.*

clad in a mantle of snow.

The next stage of the walk is a pleasant romp along the northern shoulder of Skythorn Hill to Upper Glendevon Reservoir, which can be glimpsed ahead. Although well away from civilization by this time, the Ochils have a very friendly feel to them. This is the remotest section of the walk and you are unlikely to meet anyone else, especially if you choose a weekday for your outing.

The reservoir ❸ dam is a good place to pause for a picnic. If you have brought along a pair of binoculars — and this is strongly recommended — you can take a closer look at the ducks and waders on the water and the small islands in its midst. Mallard, curlew and oystercatcher are amongst the birds to look out for. The reservoir is one of two in the glen, Lower Glendevon Reservoir being the companion in this water catchment scheme.

COVERED BY WATER

The reservoirs do not diminish the beauty of the surroundings. The original trade route followed by the weavers is covered by the water. With the reservoir behind you, the big hills further north become visible again and the village of Blackford comes into view, set in the flat farmland of Perthshire. The big white building of Tullibardane Distillery is prominent here. Blackford is a quiet place where, no doubt, the Tillicoultry weavers would have sought refreshment before selling their wares, and you can do the same. Today, apart from

The Tillicoultry Weavers

The Clackmannanshire hillfoot towns of Menstrie, Alva, Tillicoultry and Dollar have a long history of weaving. Before the Industrial Revolution, the majority of people gained a living from farming small settlements. They needed clothing, so they spun and wove the wool of their sheep into loose cloth, which was hard-wearing and warm.

More was produced than local people required for their own needs and the surplus was traded. The cloth they made became known as Tillicoultry Serge. Large quantities of finer wool were imported from Edinburgh and the south as trade developed, so that by the 1830s the plainer, coarser goods were superseded by higher-quality tartans — in particular shawls, which became the staple trade of the area.

The preparatory work of carding and spinning was carried out by women and children, but men did the weaving because wooden handlooms took a great deal of physical strength to use.

By the end of the 18th century, there was an increasing demand for cloth from the expanding towns and cities of central Scotland. Mechanization was introduced, mills were built and the shift from home-based production to a factory-based system gathered momentum. A ready supply of running water, from the burns that rushed forcefully down the steep hillsides, provided power. Steam engines eventually took over, powered by a conveniently local source of coal.

By the middle of the 19th century, with the invention of powered looms, mechanization and the factory system really took hold. In 1869, over 2,000 people were employed in 12 woollen mills, and the value of cloth woven in that year

The burn running alongside Clock Mill was used as a natural source of power to assist in the operation of heavy machinery.

was estimated at over £100,000. Mechanized weaving no longer required strength, and women superseded men in this work.

A sharp decline in the industry by the mid-20th century meant that there were fewer jobs available, while for those with steady work conditions were much better. During both World Wars, local firms produced woollen cloth for the armed forces, but later the decline continued and the family businesses disappeared.

The last weaving factory in the area, which was at Alva, closed at the end of 1990. It specialized in the production of scarves and rugs. The decline in weaving gave momentum to an expansion in the knitwear trade, and several old mill buildings now house machinery for making designer woollens.

▶ *A drystone wall zigzags through the valley. There are still, occasionally, minor earth tremors in this area.*

the whisky distillery, the Highland Spring mineral water plant provides some local employment. The ancient trading links with Tillicoultry have long since disappeared.

CENTRAL

GLYN SATTERLEY. INSET: GEOFF DORÉ/BRUCE COLEMAN LTD

A forest walk to old slate quarries and lovely waterfalls

The village of Aberfoyle is situated on the line of the Highland Boundary Fault, which separates Highland Scotland from the Lowlands. This is an excellent base from which to explore the delights of the Trossachs. An area of knobbly mountains, lochs and forested slopes, it was made famous by Sir Walter Scott, whose well-known novel *Rob Roy* and epic poem *The Lady of the Lake* were set here. Notable among the many hotels and guest houses in the village is the Baillie Nicol Jarvie, which has close associations with the real-life Rob Roy, a Scottish freebooter.

HUGE FOREST

To the north lies the 42,000-acre (17,000-ha) Queen Elizabeth Forest Park, a huge area in which the Forestry Commission has largely succeeded in combining commercial

FACT FILE

* Aberfoyle, 20 miles (32km) north of Glasgow

* Pathfinder 369 (NN 40/50), grid reference NN 519014

miles 0 1 2 3 4 5 6 7 8 9 10 miles
kms 0 1 2 3 4 5 6 7 8 9 10 11 12 13 14 15 kms

* Allow 3 hours

* Not suitable for the elderly or for young children. A steep climb at the start of the walk. Path can be very muddy and walking boots are essential. Caution is needed near quarries

* **P** Public car park at David Marshall Lodge (small fee)

* Tea room in David Marshall Lodge (closed on weekdays in winter). Cafés, fish and chips, restaurants and pubs 1 mile (1.6km) from start in Aberfoyle

* **WC** In David Marshall Lodge and Aberfoyle

▲*Across the loch near David Marshall Lodge there is a fine view of the wooded Trossachs. The caterpillar of the northern eggar moth (inset) feeds on heather and brambles in these hills.*

forestry with recreation. There are many fine waymarked paths here for walkers and cyclists, and even some special motorist's routes.

At the south side of the Park, on a hillside above Aberfoyle, stands David Marshall Lodge **Ⓐ**. This was built by the Carnegie Trust, of which David Marshall was chairman, as a viewpoint and picnic area. In 1960, it was presented to the Forestry Commission, who now use it as an information centre for the Park.

DISTANT HILLS

Beyond the low-lying lands that surround the young River Forth, the Campsie Fells and Kilpatrick Hills are visible in the distance. To the north-west of the lodge, on the outward leg of the walk, the hills of Craigmore and Creag a' Mhadaidh are broken up by large quarries. These old slate quarries **Ⓑ** were once

THE WALK

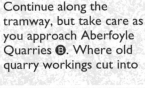

Continue along the tramway, but take care as you approach Aberfoyle Quarries **B**. Where old quarry workings cut into

6 At the cottage, turn right (with Duke's Pass **C** over to your left) and follow the main road for a few minutes.

7 At the start of the wayfaring course, turn left into the forest and follow the forest track. Bear right, then turn right at a forest road junction. Continue on the road, passing a small quarry before a bend curves to the left.

8 At a crossroads, turn right and follow the road downhill, to walk through a small valley, with a burn on your left. Continue, crossing over the burn, passing some fine waterfalls **D** where the burn meets Allt a' Mhangam.

9 At a marker post, turn right. Re-enter the valley of the burn and continue through some oak and holly woods, following the burn downstream until you pass a large waterfall.

10 Cross the footbridge below the waterfall. Turn right and follow the trails to return to David Marshall Lodge car park.

DAVID MARSHALL LODGE – ABERFOYLE QUARRIES

The starting point of the walk is the car park of David Marshall Lodge **A**.

1 Take the main exit from David Marshall Lodge, turn right onto the main road and take the second small path off to the left, about 50 yards (45m) from the lodge on a bend, to head north, uphill.

2 Follow the path uphill, ignoring a level track that crosses the path. About 50 yards (45m) beyond this, cross a stile over a low fence and continue.

3 You soon reach the old tramway (identifiable from the surrounding slate) and the path veers right to become straighter and more level. Beware of erosion in places.

4 Cross a stile into the forestry plantation. Beware of boggy ground and fallen trees on this section.

the track, pick your way around them by going through the trees.

5 At the main entrance to the quarries, turn right and join the access road to Hill Cottage. The slate in the quarry tends to be unstable, particularly after rain, and it is unwise to scramble about in the quarry itself.

the third largest of their type in Scotland and provided considerable employment in Aberfoyle. A tramway was built to link them to the railway in the village. As well as slate mining, Aberfoyle once had a thriving iron smelting industry, and the station yard must then have been a noisy, bustling place.

A PRETTY PASS

A little further round the route, the walk takes you across Duke's Pass **C**, which was named after the Duke of Montrose, the 17th-century Royalist Scottish general, who once swore to protect the Presbyterian

◀ The view from beside Allt a' Mhangam burn, looking back to Hill Cottage and Duke's Pass to the right.

Church from attempted Anglican reforms. The pass was once the scene of intense combat. In 1651, General Monck, Oliver Cromwell's commander in Scotland, tried to subdue the Royalist forces there. Trouble flared again two years later, when the Earl of Glencairn and Graham of Duchray ambushed Monck's men, this time routing the Cromwellian force.

THE WAY HOME

On the final section of the walk, there is a beautiful babbling burn, and some fine waterfalls **D**, particularly where the burn runs into Allt a' Mhangam, which means 'the stream of the little fawn'. Finally the route leads you back through more woods to David Marshall Lodge.

Strolling through mixed woodland to visit two castles

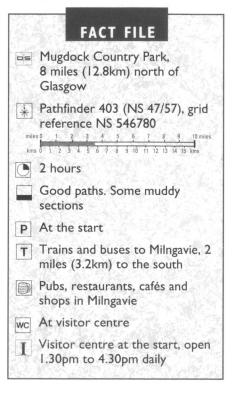

GORDON THOMSON/SCOTLAND IN FOCUS. INSET: D. BURROWS/SCOTLAND IN FOCUS

Mugdock Country Park **A** is an area of woodland, marshes, lochs and pastures just 10 miles (16km) by road from the centre of Glasgow. It boasts a network of good footpaths and bridleways, a team of countryside rangers to provide information and a programme of guided walks. There are also adventure playgrounds, picnic areas and barbecue sites.

PHEASANT'S WOOD

The walk begins at the visitor centre and heads straight into Pheasant's Wood **B**, a relatively newly planted area of young birch. At the far side of the wood is a marshy area where rhododendrons bloom in late spring. The route then heads across the open ground of Peitch's Moor, and there are good views over Mugdock Loch **C**.

After descending from the moor, the walk skirts around the loch to arrive at Mugdock Castle **D**, occupying a raised site on its western shore. The castle was built in the 14th century by the Graham family, who did great service for Scotland in the continuing struggle with England.

A centre of local power until the 17th century, the castle was sacked by Parliamentary forces when the Grahams sided with Charles I in the Civil War. Though rebuilt, on a smaller scale, the site never regained its former importance.

CASTLE RESTORATIONS

A walled garden and a summerhouse were added around 1820, and further demolition and rebuilding took place later in the century before the castle was eventually abandoned. It is now a ruin, in the process of being restored, but the 14th-century wall and south-west tower remain impressive features.

Beyond the castle is Mugdock Wood **E**, an ancient broadleaved woodland of oak, alder, ash, elm and rowan. The area has been listed as a Site of Special Scientific Interest. Beyond the wood, the route picks up a section of the West Highland

▲*Ruined Mugdock Castle, which overlooks Mugdock Loch, was the family seat of the Grahams. Fairy foxglove (inset) is a garden escape which grows on the castle walls.*

FACT FILE

⌖	Mugdock Country Park, 8 miles (12.8km) north of Glasgow
✳	Pathfinder 403 (NS 47/57), grid reference NS 546780

miles 0 1 2 3 4 5 6 7 8 9 10 miles
kms 0 1 2 3 4 5 6 7 8 9 10 11 12 13 14 15 kms

◔	2 hours
▬	Good paths. Some muddy sections
P	At the start
T	Trains and buses to Milngavie, 2 miles (3.2km) to the south
🍴	Pubs, restaurants, cafés and shops in Milngavie
WC	At visitor centre
I	Visitor centre at the start, open 1.30pm to 4.30pm daily

THE WALK

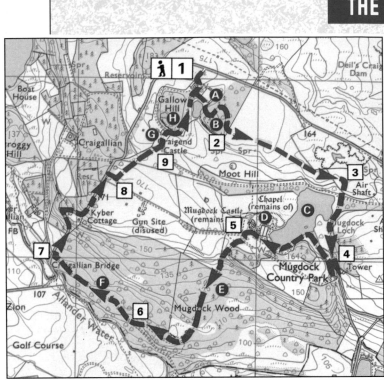

GALLOW HILL – MUGDOCK WOOD

The walk begins at Craigend Visitor Centre. Driving from Milngavie, follow a minor road signposted 'Mugdock' that leaves the B8030 in the centre of town. Alternatively, you can walk to the park along the signposted West Highland Way from the BR station in Milngavie and join the walk at stage 6.

1 Go to the left of the visitor centre into Mugdock Country Park **A**, taking the path that descends to a pond ahead. Halfway along the far side of the pond, turn left and climb some steps that lead you into Pheasant's Wood **B**. At a fork just above the steps, go left along a path winding among the young birch trees. The path encircles the wood and reaches a marshy corner where it turns to the right and goes through some rhododendrons. On the left, immediately before the corner, two paths through a thin belt of trees become grassy paths going across Peitch's Moor.

2 Take the first, left-hand path, which crosses the centre of the moor. A marked bridleway joins from the right and, a little further along, branches off to the left. Ignore this and continue straight on, crossing another marked bridleway.

3 About 100 yards (90m) beyond the second bridleway, just after climbing a short rise, branch sharp right on a small path that descends to a crossroads at the corner of Mugdock Loch **C**. Cross straight over, following the track signposted 'South Lodge'.

4 At a fork keep right, to cross a bridleway and a bridge. At a junction, turn right on a track that is signposted 'Mugdock Castle', which leads along the shores of Mugdock Loch to the castle **D**.

5 At a crossroads on the far side of Mugdock Castle, bend left then turn right at a fork, following a path signposted 'Mugdock Wood'. The path crosses a bridleway and a field to a gate at the entrance to Mugdock Wood **E**. Go through the gate and keep to the main path as it descends into the wood, crosses a marshy area on a wooden walkway and bears right to reach a junction with the waymarked West Highland Way **F**.

6 Bear right along the West Highland Way. After 660 yards (600m) you come to a road.

7 Turn right and follow the road uphill around a hairpin bend. Above the bend, the road levels out. Follow a track on your right, signposted 'Kyber Car Park', for about 50 paces to reach a gate in the fence on your left.

8 Go through the gate and take a path signposted 'Visitor Centre' that leads to a junction beside Craigend Castle **G**.

9 Turn left at the junction, then take a track that climbs to the right of Gallow Hill **H** to return to the visitor centre.

Way **F**. This long-distance path links Milngavie with Fort William 95 miles (152km) to the north. It was officially opened in 1980 as Scotland's first official long-distance footpath and is now enjoyed by an estimated 60,000 walkers a year.

ON THE WAY

After following the Way through woodland, the route turns right up a minor road to visit Craigend Castle **G**. Unlike Mugdock Castle, this is not a genuine medieval building, but a Gothic fantasy, with octagonal, square and circular towers complete with embrasures and corbels.

In 1670 the Smith family, as a reward for their longstanding, loyal service as blacksmiths and armourers to the Graham armies, were allowed to buy the land on which the castle now stands. Their descendants built Craigend Castle in 1816. Craigend stables, which now house the visitor centre, were built at around the same time.

The last of the Smith lairds died in 1851, and the castle became home to a string of owners and tenants. Between 1949 and 1956 it was the centre of a zoo that claimed to have the 'biggest rat in the world', as well as Charlie, 'the largest elephant in captivity'. The castle is now a shell.

As you head back to the start of the walk, you skirt the eastern flank of Gallow Hill **H**, where public executions took place until 1800.

▶ *One of the attractions of the park is an endearing herd of shaggy-coated, short-horned Highland cattle.*

GORDON THOMSON/SCOTLAND IN FOCUS

TENTSMUIR SANDS

Where the walk begins is a good place to look for the rare lady's tresses orchid. Birds abound among the pines, and a little quiet observation will pay dividends. Particularly common is the coal tit, which likes coniferous woodland and is easily identified. Also look out for squirrels, rabbits and roe deer.

FROZEN FISH

The first of two ponds encountered on the route is Heron Pond **B**, which the Forestry Commission has developed to improve the habitat for wildlife. Unfortunately for the birds, the pond can dry out completely if there is not much rain.

At the most northerly point of the walk is the ice house **D** and its neighbouring pond **C**. At the end of the 19th century an attempt was made to introduce salmon fishing here on a commercial basis. The pond was used to produce ice,

A deserted beach and shoreline forest

This stretch of coastline in south-east Scotland is home to sea birds and seals, and the forest fringes the shoreline. The walk begins beside the deserted beach where the opening scene of *Chariots of Fire* was filmed, and continues into Tentsmuir Forest which is rich with its own wildlife.

The forest was acquired by the Forestry Commission in the early 1920s. Planting started in 1922 and since then the forest has grown to its present size of around 3,950 acres (1600 hectares). The plantations in this area are mostly of Scots and Corsican pine and Tentsmuir Forest contains some majestic specimens of these trees.

Planted on sand dunes between the estuaries of the Rivers Tay and Eden, Tentsmuir derives its name from old writings which describe fishermen pitching their tents on the dunes or 'muir' (heath).

HAVEN FOR WILDLIFE

The plantations and their surrounds provide a habitat for a wide diversity of plant and animal life. Next to

▲ *A wide, unspoilt beach, Tentsmuir Sands, bordered by Tentsmuir Forest (below), is often inhabited only by seals and sea birds. (inset) Grass of Parnassus likes marshy ground.*

the car park where the walk starts is Tentsmuir Sands **A**. This coastline, with its high sand dunes, includes a national nature reserve. Swimming is not advisable due to strong underwater currents.

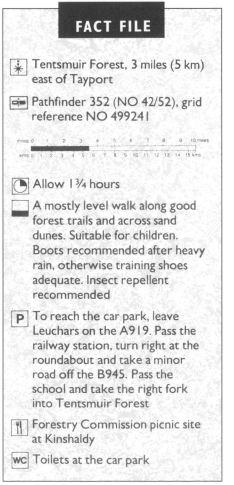

STEVE COOPER. INSET: DAVID WOODFALL/NHPA

STEVE COOPER

FIFE

FACT FILE

⚓ Tentsmuir Forest, 3 miles (5 km) east of Tayport

▭ Pathfinder 352 (NO 42/52), grid reference NO 499241

miles 0 1 2 3 4 5 6 7 8 9 10 miles
kms 0 1 2 3 4 5 6 7 8 9 10 11 12 13 14 15 kms

◔ Allow 1¾ hours

▬ A mostly level walk along good forest trails and across sand dunes. Suitable for children. Boots recommended after heavy rain, otherwise training shoes adequate. Insect repellent recommended

P To reach the car park, leave Leuchars on the A919. Pass the railway station, turn right at the roundabout and take a minor road off the B945. Pass the school and take the right fork into Tentsmuir Forest

🍴 Forestry Commission picnic site at Kinshaldy

WC Toilets at the car park

THE WALK

TENTSMUIR FOREST - TENTSMUIR NATURE RESERVE

The walk begins at the Forestry Commission picnic site in the forest.

1 At the far end of the car park walk towards the beach and locate a marker post indicating the start of the outward route. Leave the beach **A** and take the sandy path between an avenue of trees. The path becomes slightly firmer as you progress and the way is obvious, though marker posts will confirm the correct route.

2 Where the path divides there are two marker posts. Follow the one to the left. After a few yards, on your right is another marker post, across a small ditch (be careful not to miss this one). A stream runs beside the path. Continue on the forest trail until a wooden bridge comes into view. Over this on the right, among the trees, is the Heron Pond **B**.

3 Cross back over the bridge and take the marker post ahead. In a short distance the path

emerges on a forestry road. Turn right along this for a short way until another marker post on the left leads you back into deciduous woodland along a cleared trail. Continue, following the trail to reach two marker posts at a gap in the trees – one left and one right. Take the left path to a hide overlooking the ice house pond, which is now called Tentsmuir Pond **C** Retrace your steps.

4 Take the path on the right which leads on to the forestry road which you left earlier. Ignoring a marker post on the right which leads back into the pines, look to the left to find a dome-roofed building. This is the ice house **D**.

5 Behind the ice house on a track just to the right of the building is a gate with a stile on its left. A sign indicates that you are entering Tentsmuir Point National Nature Reserve, **E** where seals can usually be seen. Cross the stile and take a good track through birchwoods to the point, where there is an observation tower

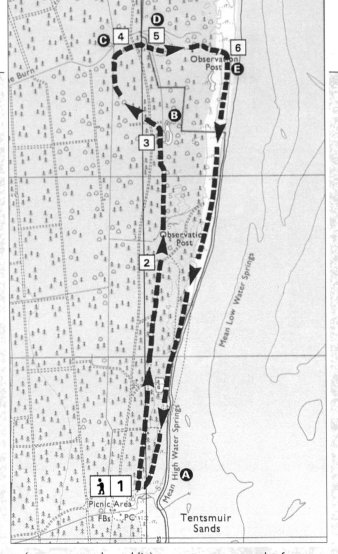

(not open to the public).

6 Having drunk your fill of the superb seascape and the wildlife, turn right to follow sandy paths through the dunes, with the beach and sea on your left, all the way back to the start. Alternatively, you

can re-enter the forest where there is a hexagonal concrete plinth (the base of a building) on the right. A marker post on the track just behind it indicates the direction. Further on, easily followed posts lead back to the car park through the pines.

▲ *Tentsmuir Pond, now a place for spotting wildlife, previously supplied ice for the ice house (right). The two-tier, stone building remains dark and cold.*

which was then stored in the ice house to preserve the fish. The enterprise did not last long, but both the pond and ice house remain

as a legacy of the failed project. There is now a hide at the pond so visitors can watch the wildlife.

After leaving the forest the scene changes completely, with the dunes forming the fringe of Tentsmuir Point National Nature Reserve **E**. Beyond the beach, on the water's edge, waders sift through the sand for food. The cries of gulls and the haunting call of the curlew fill the air. Further out on the sandbars, seals can frequently be seen; both the common and grey species. Large numbers of sea duck winter just offshore, particularly eider. A pair of binoculars is especially useful for viewing the birds and seals.

K. KEANE/SCOTLAND IN FOCUS. INSET: DAVID OVERCASH/BRUCE COLEMAN LTD

▲*The remains of the fortified castle of St Andrews dominate the town. Its commanding position helped guard the bay and countryside. Daisies (left) grow in short grassland nearby.*

From the home of golf to Scotland's oldest university

St Andrews is beautifully situated in a sheltered bay on the coast of Fife. It is a town of great character and exceptional historic interest. From at least the 6th century it was a stronghold of the Pictish kings and the site of an influential monastery of the Celtic Church. In the 8th century it became a centre for the pilgrims who came to worship the remains of St Andrew, Scotland's patron saint. The cathedral and the castle were founded in the 12th century, and Scotland's oldest university was founded at St Andrews in 1410.

Today, St Andrews is world-famous as a golfing centre, while the heart of the town has an order and dignity matched by few of the remaining medieval cities of north-western Europe. The walk explores the heart of the town, its main historical buildings and the famous golf course.

The walk starts at the car park overlooking the great sweep of West Sands Ⓐ, a superb beach stirringly

---

FACT FILE

✳ St Andrews, 11 miles (18 km) south-east of Dundee

🗺 Pathfinder 363 (NO 41/51), grid reference NO 505172

miles 0 1 2 3 4 5 6 7 8 9 10 miles
kms 0 1 2 3 4 5 6 7 8 9 10 11 12 13 14 15 kms

◔ Allow 2 to 3 hours

▬ Pavements, good paths and a sandy beach

P Large car park at start of walk

T Regular buses and trains

🍴 All facilities in town

WC At car park

🏛 Cathedral Museum open all year. British Golf Museum, Tel. (01334) 478880 for details

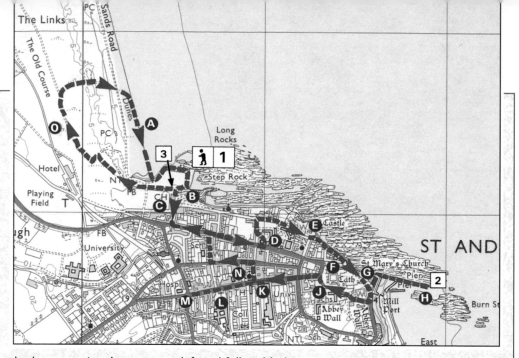

THE WALK

ST ANDREWS

The walk begins at the car park serving the British Golf Museum, opposite the Royal and Ancient Golf Club. To reach it by car, follow signs for West Sands **A**.

1 Turn left out of the car park, passing the British Golf Museum **B** on the left and the Royal and Ancient Golf Club **C** on the right. Continue up Golf Place and turn left into North Street. Continue for just over ¼ mile (400 metres) to St Salvator's **D**. Enter the quadrangle through an archway and exit through a gateway on the left side of the quadrangle. Turn right down Butts Wynd. Continue to The Scores and turn right. Follow The Scores to the castle **E**. Continue along the road until it becomes a footpath that follows the cliff top. Enter the cathedral and priory grounds **F** through a gate in the precinct wall. After exploring the grounds and climbing St Rule's Tower, return to the footpath. Follow it down the hill to the harbour, passing the remains of the Church of St Mary of the Rock **G**.

2 Walk to the end of the pier **H** then return to the harbour. Follow it round to its southern end then take a right turn up The Pends **J**, which follows the south side of the cathedral wall and finally passes through an archway. Turn left into South Street and follow this to St Mary's College **K**, Blackfriars Chapel **L** and West Port **M**. Return on the other side of South Street and turn left along Church Street, the site of Holy Trinity Church **N**. Follow Church Street to Market Street, then turn left and follow Market Street to Greyfriars Gardens. Turn right and continue to North Street. Turn left along North Street and then turn into Golf Place and arrive back at the Royal and Ancient Golf Club.

3 Turn left opposite the British Golf Museum and follow a good path for a little over ¼ mile (400 metres), with the Old Course **O** on the left, until you reach the grass at the start of the New Course, with the starter building on the right. Just before the 'New Course' signboard, go left through a gap in the gorse bushes onto the Old Course and turn right along a grassy and sandy path between the Old and New Courses. At one stage the path becomes rather indistinct, but keep straight on and it soon becomes a good gravel track. Turn right at a fork and cross the New and the Jubilee Courses (low-flying golf balls are a hazard) and follow the track to some low buildings. Beyond is another fairway. Cross it to a car park area and West Sands Road. Go over the road and the dunes and you will emerge on West Sands. Turn right along the beach and walk back to the car park.

▼*The beach at West Sands, where the walk ends, was where the runners trained in the film* **Chariots of Fire.**

K. KEANE/SCOTLAND IN FOCUS

depicted in the film *Chariots of Fire*. Near the beach is the British Golf Museum **B**, opposite the famous Royal and Ancient Golf Club **C**. Beyond the 'R & A' is the famous Old Course, where the Open Golf Championship is sometimes played.

THE UNIVERSITY

At the corner of Golf Place and North Street, the walk turns left into North Street and heads towards the centre of the old town. The main streets of St Andrews are wide and spacious with attractive, well proportioned stone buildings. The main university buildings lie halfway along North Street on the left-hand side; the ruins of the cathedral are visible at the far end of the street.

Founded in 1410, the university comprised the colleges of St Salvator's **D** (1450), St Leonard's (1512) and St Mary's (1537). St Salvator's and St Leonard's were amalgamated in 1747 to form United College. The entrance to St Salvator's is through an archway with heavy wooden doors that lead to a large quadrangle with well-kept lawns. Initials on the pavement in front of the archway mark the spot where Patrick Hamilton was burned at the stake in 1528 for teaching Lutheran doctrines. He was the first martyr of the Scottish Reformation. There is a superstition among students today that to set foot on the initials will mean doing badly in university examinations.

A gate exits from the spacious quadrangle into Butts Wynd, a

▲*St Salvator's is one of the three original university colleges.The university was founded in 1410.*

narrow street leading to The Scores, a quiet road shaded by trees, with many university departments in the buildings on either side.

THE CASTLE

Soon the castle **E** is reached. It dates from about 1200 and was at one time the principal residence of the Bishops of St Andrews. Protected on its north and east sides by high cliffs and the sea, it was once a formidable fortress and prison. The fascinating mine and counter-mine are a rare example of medieval siege technique, and the castle is also famous for its bottle dungeon, hollowed out of solid rock.

From here the walk follows the cliff top towards the grounds of the cathedral **F**, which are entered by a

small gateway in the precinct wall. The cathedral was founded in 1160, while the ancient priory here dates from the 13th century. Despite the destructive efforts of the Reformation, the remains of the cathedral still give a vivid impression of the massive scale of what was once the largest church in the whole of Scotland.

ST RULE'S TOWER

In the grounds there is a visitor centre, where tickets are available for the museum and an ascent of St Rule's Tower. The museum has a collection of Celtic and medieval artefacts, including a superb sarcophagus that dates from the 8th or 10th century. Legend maintains that St Rule (also known as St Regulus) brought the relics of St Andrew to

Fife. A church was built about 1130, but today only the choir and the tower remain. A steep ascent by spiral steps leads to the top of the 108-foot (33-metre) tower, from which there is a magnificent view over St Andrews and the surrounding coast and hills.

Returning to the cliff path, the route descends towards the harbour, passing the Church of St Mary of the Rock **G**. Only the foundations now remain of this Celtic settlement, which was perched on the cliff above the harbour. It fell into disuse as the Church of St Rule and the cathedral prospered.

During term-time, the harbour is the site of a colourful tradition after the Sunday morning service at St Salvator's Chapel, as the students embark on their customary walk

▲*Much of the damage done to the now-ruined St Andrews Cathedral was inflicted on it during the Reformation in the 16th century. The harbour at St Andrews (left) is a popular port of call for small pleasure cruisers.*

along the pier **H**, wearing red gowns. The pier was constructed with stones from the ruins of the castle and the cathedral.

Leaving the harbour, the route returns to the town centre by following Pends Road beside the old wall of the cathedral. The wall is about 1 mile (1.6 km) long and was mainly built in the early 16th century. At the top, the road passes through The Pends **J**, a 14th-century vaulted gatehouse that formed the main entrance to the priory.

BOTH PHOTOS PETER DAVENPORT/EDINBURGH PHOTO LIBRARY

▲ *The greystone buildings of St Andrews give way to the open spaces of the golf links and the coast.*

From The Pends, South Street leads through the town to West Port, the main entrance to the old town of St Andrews, with several interesting buildings on the way. Just around the corner from The Pends is Queen Mary's House, a 16th-century house where Mary Queen of Scots is reputed to have stayed. Halfway along South Street is St Mary's College **K**, founded in 1537. It now houses the Faculty of Divinity. As you enter the quadrangle of St Mary's, there is a striking view of a magnificent holm oak, which was planted in 1728.

TOWN CENTRE

A little further along is the tourist information office and the town hall, which was built in 1858. Continuing towards West Port, there are the remains of Blackfriars Chapel **L**. All that is left of this small Dominican church is a spectacular single apse.

The West Port **M**, at the west end of South Street, is one of the few surviving city gates in Scotland. It was built in 1580 and still serves as a thoroughfare. From here the walk crosses to the other side of South Street, which forms, with Market Street, the main shopping area of St Andrews. Reaching Church Street, there is the Holy Trinity Church **N**, which is the town kirk, dating from 1410. Church Street leads to the focal point of Market Street, the Mercat Cross, the original cross now replaced by a fountain.

GOLF LINKS

Soon you return to the Old Course **O**, and its first tee just in front of the 'R & A'. A westward path heads over the 500 acres (200 hectares) of golf links that lie to the north-west of St Andrews. About ½ mile (800 metres) along this path, a track eastwards crosses the New Course and the Jubilee Course to West Sands Road. Beyond the road, small sand dunes back the huge expanse of West Sands. The last section of the walk is along the beach, heading southwards towards the town of St Andrews and the car park.

The Home of Golf

Golf has been played in Fife since the 15th century or even earlier. In 1457 James II, King of Scots, banned the game so men would concentrate on their archery practice. Later, in 1567, Mary Queen of Scots played here. Today, St Andrews is internationally famous as the traditional home of this long-established sport.

The Royal and Ancient Golf Club was founded in 1754, acquiring its royal title in 1834 when King William IV was nominated as patron of the club. The clubhouse dates from 1854 and is recognized as the headquarters of world golf. Nearby is the British Golf Museum.

There are 15 golf courses in north-east Fife, including the legendary Old Course at St Andrews. This has been the site of 24 Open Championships, as well as many other professional and amateur events, including the Ryder Cup played between teams from Europe and the USA. With a par of 72, the 6,566 yards (5,995 metres) are a great test for any golfer, especially on a windy day. The nearby New Course was laid out in 1895, two years before the Jubilee Course, which commemorates the 60th year of Queen Victoria's reign.

To the cheers of the crowd, many great golfers have strode across this bridge on their way to the 18th green and victory.

THE SCOTTISH RIVIERA

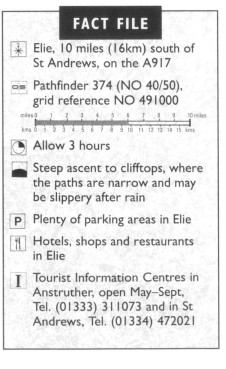

◀*Sturdy stone walls buttress the gardens of houses at Elie Harbour. The hermit crab (inset), which adopts the empty shells of shellfish, lives in rock pools and coastal waters.*

noble ladies of Elie House **B**.

The house, the ancestral home of the Anstruther family since 1366, includes remnants of an L-shaped towerhouse that was built by Sir William Anstruther in 1697. The most celebrated of the house's former inhabitants was Janet Fall, who married Sir John Anstruther in 1750 and was immortalized by Thomas Carlyle as 'a coquette and a beauty'.

A CURSE

In spite, or perhaps because, of her lowly birth, Lady Janet proved an insufferable snob. Taking a strong dislike to the neighbouring village of Balclevie, which was inhabited by tinkers, she had it demolished 'to improve the view'. A 'spey-wifie' (fortune teller) from the condemned hamlet cursed the family and foretold that only six generations of Anstruthers would live in the house. Her prediction proved true, and Elie House is now a convent.

Returning to the town, you follow a narrow, meandering wynd

Two historic towns on a coastline of cliffs and sandy beaches

The towns of Earlsferry and Elie lie side by side along the wide arc of a south-facing bay, from which there are extensive views along the rugged coast of the Firth of Forth. These tiny towns have ancient roots, with their histories dating back through the first Jacobite Rebellion (1689) to the real-life King Macbeth in the 11th century.

The walk begins in the tree-lined town square of Elie. The town's economy once thrived on fishing, boat-building and weaving, but its current prosperity stems from the fine golf links and the golden sands.

The route initially heads inland, through a corridor of riotously coloured, semi-wild rhododendrons, towards Elie House. Just to your east is a striking folly **A**. The monument's origins are obscure. It bears no inscription, simply a plaque of a horse's head; it is thought to commemorate either an Elie racehorse, or a favourite hunter of one of the

---

FACT FILE

✳ Elie, 10 miles (16km) south of St Andrews, on the A917

▱ Pathfinder 374 (NO 40/50), grid reference NO 491000

miles 0 1 2 3 4 5 6 7 8 9 10 miles
kms 0 1 2 3 4 5 6 7 8 9 10 11 12 13 14 15 kms

◔ Allow 3 hours

◗ Steep ascent to clifftops, where the paths are narrow and may be slippery after rain

🅿 Plenty of parking areas in Elie

🍴 Hotels, shops and restaurants in Elie

ℹ Tourist Information Centres in Anstruther, open May–Sept, Tel. (01333) 311073 and in St Andrews, Tel. (01334) 472021

THE WALK

ELIE – SHELL BAY

The starting point of the walk is in the parking area in Elie High Street.

1 Head east along the High Street, past the Town Square, to the de-restriction signs. Turn left through a double-arched entrance. Follow the driveway, past a monument **A** on your right, to Elie House **B**. Retrace your steps to the main road and turn right.

2 Take the first turning left. Follow this road as it bears right to a T-junction at Elie Harbour.

3 Turn right on the harbour road, then take the next turning left. At a crossroads, go straight on into South Street **C**. At the end of the street, continue along the beach, following the shore to Earlsferry.

4 At the harbour wall, turn right up the steps, between the houses onto a tarmac road. Turn left and follow the road to join a grassy path, passing a ruin **D** on your left. Continue onto the golf course **E**. At a T-junction of paths, turn left towards the bay.

5 Turn right along the narrow path bordering the golf course. (Alternatively, walk parallel to this path, along the beach, towards the cliffs **F**.) At the end of the bay, bear right onto a dirt path winding uphill to the clifftops.

6 At a ruined building, bear left and follow the narrow clifftop path. Beyond the mast, bear left on a broad track. After 100 yards (90m), where the main track bends right, continue straight on along a narrower path leading around the headland. Follow the path past ruined buildings to some steps on your left, which lead to the raised beaches **G**. Descend two flights of steps, and follow a dirt path around Shell Bay.

7 Cross a footbridge and turn right to join a tarmac road. Take the first turning right and go ahead to a T-junction. Turn right onto a farm road. Where another farm road crosses, turn left. Continue past the ruins of the Grange **H** on your left.

8 At the end of some houses, turn left along a rough road skirting the golf course. At a T-junction, turn right onto a tarmac road. At a crossroads, turn left. Follow the road back to Elie, passing the parish church **J** on your left, to return to the car park.

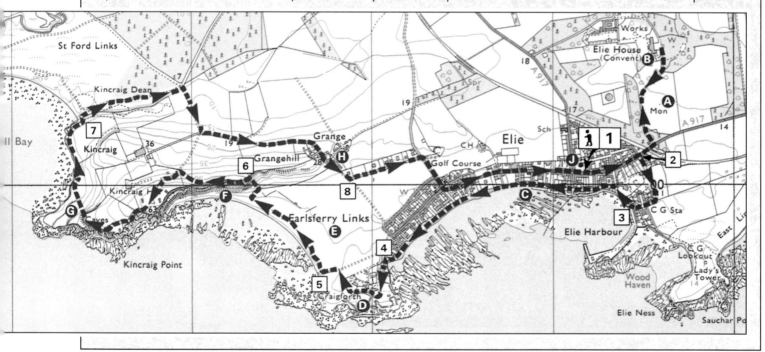

(alley) down to Elie Harbour, which was established in 1586. In 1715, the Earl of Mar landed in this natural haven and, joined by several sympathetic Fife lairds, raised the Jacobite standard. A few months later, the Earl returned to Elie to lead his Highland Army across the Forth and into bloody battle.

The houses along the deep, golden bay have high walls, which

◀ *This stone doorway and old timber door were the entrance to a sawpit.*

act as buttresses against surging tides. In winter, sea spray lashes the windows and wind-blown sands drift along the pavements of South Street **C**. Here, in the oldest part of the town, the characterful houses have elegant crow-stepped gables and red pantile roofs.

LITHUANIAN WOOD

The castle dates mostly from the early 16th century, though its tower is from the beginning of the 15th. The property was the town house of

▶ *Apart from its harbour, Elie has two main attractions, the beach and the golf course. The wide sands of the beach (right) stretch westwards from the harbour. Inland from the beach and running further west are Earlsferry Links (below right), one of the Fife coast's famous courses.*

the Gourlays of Kincraig. Almost opposite is a weather-beaten timber door. This was once the entrance to a sawpit, where wood brought to Elie Harbour from Klaipeda, in Lithuania, was cut.

CISTERCIAN RUIN

The path along the bay leads into Earlsferry, a Royal burgh founded by Alexander II in 1223. The island of Chapel Ness, which was formerly the headland here, takes its name from a chapel ❶ that was run by the Cistercian nuns of North Berwick. Its forlorn ruin stands on a site that had been occupied since 1093.

Those who made the often-treacherous crossing north over the Firth of Forth used to disembark at Earlsferry. In the Middle Ages, the nuns set up lamps to light the way 'for the solace of weary and storm-tossed travellers', many of whom were pilgrims on their way to St Andrews. Today, the automated beacon of East Vows warns pleasure boats away from the sea-washed, rocky islands of Chapel Ness and East and West Vows.

As you look east from the headland, the ruins of the Lady's Tower are visible above Elie Harbour. Built in the 18th century, the tower was used as a changing-room by the ravishingly beautiful (if vain) Lady Janet. When she took to the sea, a bellman walked the village streets warning peasants to keep away.

As the route continues, the path runs alongside the golf course ❷, which claims to have a sporting history dating back to the 16th century. James Braid, five times Open Champion between 1901 and 1910,

was Earlsferry's most famous golfing son. He was the first player to score below 300 for 72 holes at St Andrews' Old Course, and ranked alongside Harry Vardon and J H Taylor as the greatest British golfers of the Edwardian era.

ABUNDANT FLORA

The fringes of the links are carpeted with kidney vetch, yarrow, sea-rocket, bird's-foot trefoil, thyme and eyebright. Butterflies thrive in this unpolluted habitat, and the small heath, common blue and the colourful cinnabar moth are widespread. Warm rock pools along the shore support an exotic range of sea creatures. Well camouflaged shrimps, sea-anemones and hermit, edible and dark-green shore crabs scuttle beneath rocks festooned with seaweed. The dunes are alive with

▶ *The varied local coastline features sandy beaches, rock pools and, as here, to the west of Earlsferry, jagged cliffs.*

meadow rue, milk vetch, rockrose and sweet-scented burnet rose, all of which flourish on the sandy soil.

The cliffs ❸ beyond the links are arguably the finest in Scotland, with spectacular basalt pillars and caves. At the foot is the Chain Walk; steps cut into the rock-face and a handrail of chains provide a fascinating, if hazardous, ascent, though the route is impassable at high tide. The

◀ *The view west to Shell Bay, where there are raised beaches, with Largo Bay in the distance.*

JASON SMALLEY

largest cave provided a welcome hiding place for Macduff (Shakespeare's Thane of Fife) as he fled from the very real Macbeth, an 11th-century Scottish king. A local fisherman ferried Earl Macduff across the Firth of Forth to safety, earning the town its name.

On the clifftops are remnants of wartime gun emplacements. To the west of Kincraig Point are raised beaches ❼ on three levels. These wide plateaux, 100 feet (30m), 50 feet (15m) and 25 feet (7.5m) high, lead to Shell Bay. The terraces mark the levels of the sea as the land rose on the retreat of the glaciers at the end of the last Ice Age.

Gulls, terns, cormorants, fulmars, shags and gannets bob about in the current, and brilliant clumps of field poppies, sea campion and agrimony add splashes of colour to the grassy slopes, together with the pink buds and bright blue flowers of viper's bugloss — once thought to be a cure for snake bites. Beyond here is the larger crescent of Largo Bay. In the distance is Largo Law, an extinct volcano that rises to 952 feet (290m).

The road behind the golf course leads east to the ruins of the old Grange ❽. Established by the nuns of North Berwick, it was run as a hospice for travellers using ferries across the Forth. To the right of the track, a deep depression crossing the links marks the route of Cadger's Road, along which carriers trundled their wagons of fish bound for the Royal Palaces of Falkland.

HANDSOME BELLTOWER

The footpath through Earlsferry leads back to Elie and the parish church ❾, built by Sir William Scott of Ardross Castle in the 1630s. The rather distinguished campanile was added by Sir John Anstruther in 1726. An interesting tombstone, set in the east wall of the church and dedicated to the daughter of Thomas Turnbull of Bogmill, depicts a macabre, full-sized skeleton, which is swathed from shoulder to ankles in a scrolled shroud.

▼ *Tombstone in the church wall at Elie.*

JASON SMALLEY

Castaway

MARY EVANS PICTURE LIBRARY

Robinson Crusoe encounters with astonishment a footprint in the sand which will lead him to Man Friday.

privateering expedition as Sailing Master of the *Cinque Ports*. The ship's captain died, and Lieutenant Thomas Stradling took command.

The new captain proved unequal to the role, and there were mutinous murmurings among the crew. Having little confidence in the ship's future, Selkirk asked to be put ashore. When the *Cinque Ports* reached the island of Juan Fernandez, he was landed with his sea-chest, mathematical instruments, Bible, kettle, hatchet and gun. His decision was prudent; the ship subsequently foundered off the Peruvian coast with the loss of all but eight lives.

Over four years later, the famous sea captain Woodes Rogers moored off Juan Fernandez. Seeing a light ashore, he sent a boat to investigate. It returned with 'a man clothed in goat-skins, who looked wilder than the first owners of them.'

In 1711, back home in Largo, Selkirk mourned his return to the world. He believed himself to have been a better man alone on his island than he had ever been before, or would be again. In 1720 he went back to sea. On 3 December 1721, he died of yellow fever and was buried at sea off Cape Coast Castle in West Africa. *Robinson Crusoe*, inspired by the real life adventures of this voluntary castaway, was published in 1719, and became Defoe's best loved work.

During the early 18th century, Kincraig Point was a favourite haunt of Alexander Selkirk, the prototype for Daniel Defoe's *Robinson Crusoe*. On this rocky headland, Selkirk strove to recapture the isolation he had experienced after being cast away on an uninhabited island 400 miles (640km) off the coast of Chile.

Selkirk was born in 1676 in Lower Largo, Fife, the son of a shoemaker. He ran away to sea, where his aptitude for mathematics advanced his rank from ordinary seaman to navigator. In 1704, he joined a

A ROYAL VIEW

JASON SMALLEY. INSET: B. BURBIDGE/NATURE PHOTOGRAPHERS

▲*Behind the restored Falkland Palace, set in pretty gardens, rises the magnificent bulk of East Lomond, on whose grassy areas the low-spreading lady's mantle (left) can be found.*

Climb from a royal burgh to a hilltop viewpoint

Falkland, on the lower slopes of the Lomond Hills and the edge of the green and fertile Howe of Fife, has had a chequered history. It was a fortified site before the 12th century, and by the mid-15th century had become the playground of the Stuart kings, who rode out hawking with hooded falcons or hunted wild boar.

By the end of the 1700s, Falkland Palace, once a magnificent hunting lodge, was in ruins. Thomas Carlyle described it as 'a black old bit of coffin or protrusive shin-bone sticking through the soil of a dead past'. It was restored by John Crichton Stuart, 3rd Marquess of Bute, who acquired the keepership in 1887.

The castle was first adopted as a royal residence by James II, in 1458,

FACT FILE

☀ Falkland, 10miles (16km) north of Kirkcaldy, on the A912

▭ Pathfinder 373 (NO 20/30), grid reference NO 254073

miles 0 1 2 3 4 5 6 7 8 9 10 miles
kms 0 1 2 3 4 5 6 7 8 9 10 11 12 13 14 15 kms

◗ Allow 2½ hours

▬ Steep ascent and descent on the Lomond Hills. Walking boots or shoes recommended

P Free parking in centre of Falkland or on Lomond Hills at point 4 of the walk

🍴 Hotels, restaurants and shops in Falkland

WC In both car parks

⌂ Palace and gardens open Apr-Sept, Mon-Sat 10am-6pm, Sun 2-6pm; closes one hour earlier in October. Last admission one hour before closing

and the settlement around it evolved into a small but elegant market town. From it, the walk heads through beech and conifer woods, to open heather moorland managed for red grouse. Curlews, wheatears, meadow pipits, chaffinches and skylarks share the hills with the gamebirds.

The rocks of the Lomond Hills, over 350 million years old, rise to twin volcanic peaks. The brow of East Lomond **Ⓐ**, 1,424 feet (434m) above sea level, affords one of the finest views in Scotland.

SPLENDID VIEWS

The Grampians fill the north-west horizon, and, 54 miles (87km) to the west, Ben Lomond rises to a height of 3,194 feet (974m). To the east is the wide North Sea, where the lighthouses on Bell Rock and the Isle of May are clearly visible. The Firth of Forth and the Lothian shore lie to the south.

You descend steeply through huge tracts of swaying red grass. To your left, just off the main track, are 19th-century limekilns **Ⓑ**, relics of the Industrial Revolution. Stone was crushed in them and heated to make lime for mortar and for spreading on the land to increase its fertility.

THE WALK

FALKLAND – EAST LOMOND

The walk begins in the signposted car park, to the west of Falkland High Street along Back Wynd.

▶ **1** Turn left along Back Wynd. Bear right past St John's Works to the crossroads and turn left. Follow the road uphill to join a gravel path.

▶ **2** Bear right at the fork, then branch off left up the steps into woodland signposted Lomond Hills. Continue straight on uphill, out of the woodland, then bear right up the steep, distinct path to the viewpoint on the top of East Lomond Hill **A**.

▶ **3** Descend on a clear path down the opposite side. Go through a kissing gate and turn right onto the main path. Turn left after a short distance to visit the old limekilns **B**, then return to the main path and continue ahead to a T-junction with a lane.

▶ **4** Turn right and follow the lane for about 1¼ miles (2km) to Falkland town centre. Go through the Square **C** to Falkland Palace **D**. Retrace your steps along the High Street to Back Wynd. Turn left to return to the car park.

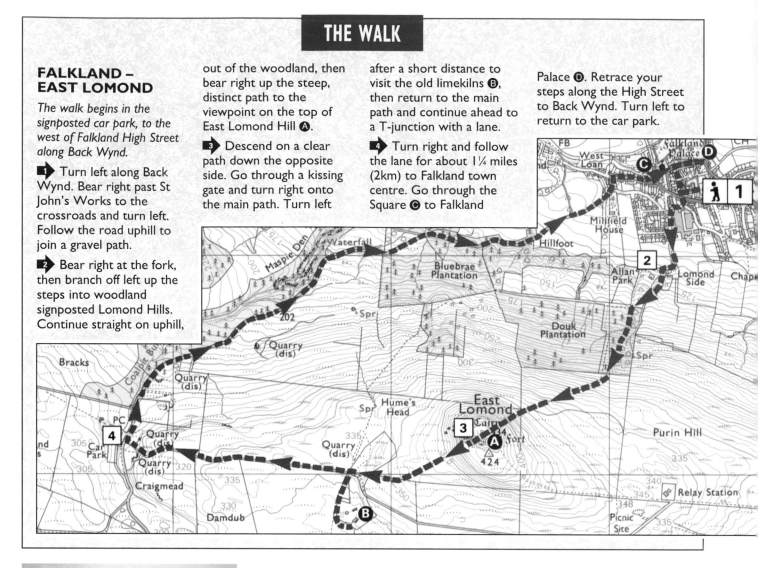

◀ *As you climb gently out of the town, there is a good view back to the church.*

A lane leads back into the town's Falkland Square **C**. The tall building on your right is Cameron House, the birthplace of Richard Cameron, the 'Lion of the Covenant'. Born in 1648, he joined the Covenanters, and was killed in 1680, fighting to overthrow Charles II.

The Gothic church was built in 1849-50 by the Keeper of the Palace at that time, Onesiphorus Tyndall Bruce, whose impressive bronze statue stands in its grounds. Another of his bequests, the handsome Bruce Fountain in front of the church, bears four heraldic lions displaying the Bruce coat of arms and the burgh crest.

CHANGES AT THE PALACE

Greatly enlarged during the reign of James IV, the palace **D** was transformed by James V during the preparation for his marriages to Madeleine, daughter of Francis I of France, who survived a mere two months of the Scottish climate, and, within a year, to her successor, Marie de Guise.

▶ *In the grounds of Falkland's church is a bronze statue erected to the memory of a former Keeper of the Palace.*

The King's Room is where James V died, shortly after hearing the news of the birth of his sole heir — Mary Queen of Scots. He turned his face to the wall, uttering a poignant prophecy on the Stuart monarchy; 'It cam wi' a lass, it will gang wi' a lass'. The prophecy proved true, if a little premature; the line ended in 1714 with the death of Queen Anne.

BOTH PHOTOS: JASON SMALLEY

INDEX